Brian Gibbs

HOW TO WIN BUYERS
AND INFLUENCE SALES WITH

facebook
ads

ESSENTIAL TIPS AND STRATEGIES FOR
GROWING YOUR BUSINESS ON FACEBOOK

HOW TO WIN BUYERS AND INFLUENCE SALES WITH FACEBOOK ADS

www.BrianGibbs.com | www.FocusedIdea.com

ISBN: 9781095702055

Imprint: Independently published

Brian Gibbs and Focused Idea focuses on total market domination for their clients to set them apart in their area and elevate their status as an industry expert and obvious choice for service.

If you are ready to take your business or practice to the next level, visit www.BrianGibbs.com or www.FocusedIdea.com and register for an in-depth marketing analysis.

Want even more?

Facebook Ads, like Facebook itself, is ever changing. Because of that, I put together a companion site with video trainings and bonuses. And, like Facebook, it will be updated as Facebook Ads change.

For my valuable readers, I am offering a discount from the membership price. All you have to do is go to facebookadsbook.briangibbs.com and enter the coupon code shown below. You'll get 25% instantly!

25% OFF!

FACEBOOKADSBOOK.BRIANGIBBS.COM

VIDEO TRAINING
& BONUSES

Coupon Code: FBADSBOOK2019

CONTENTS

FORWARD

Brian Gibbs understand what most businesses must utilize to get the best outcome from marketing. He simplified the importance of why the Facebook Ad is super beneficial, how to focus and where to begin to get started with the most critical tasks and objectives!

This is a step by step guide with images! And much more. Indeed this is an excellent gift for businesses that want to get their hands dirty enough to implement tasks that will help you get the best result you need for your business.

This book has definitely been Yusfied!

Yusuf Chowdhury, CEO & Founder at Online Business Owners

INTRODUCTION

It's very straightforward to get started with Facebook Ads. All you need is a Facebook account to create a fan page, add a method of billing, and you're ready to go. You can then start creating your ads that you can publish in just a couple of minutes or so.

You're probably thinking right now, "Wait, is that all there is to it? Is it really that simple to do Facebook ads?"

Yes, it is really is that simple if you just want to put out ads WITHOUT giving too much thought to how your audience is going to react *and* WITHOUT caring about conversions.

BUT if you're interested in creating high conversion ads at a lower cost of advertising, you need to do a lot of work.

You should know how to create a sales funnel or a lead capture funnel. For better ad engagement, you'll want to know how to target the right audiences. You will need to understand how to create the right ad creatives to catch your target audience's attention.

And if you really want to maximize your conversions, you'd have to enter the exciting world of the Facebook pixel.

It's a cute name, of course, but for any serious marketer, it's also quite possibly the best marketing tool.

So let's dive into this book, and I'll show you a few strategies on how to make Facebook ads highly converting.

CHAPTER 1: HOW TO START WITH FACEBOOK ADS

In this first chapter, you'll discover the fundamentals of Facebook Ads and how you can start with advertising on Facebook. You've probably read many success stories online of marketing professionals spending a few hundred dollars and earning returns of tens of thousands of dollars.

That seems like an insane return on investment (ROI), right? Well, not really. With Facebook Ads, it's possible to duplicate these successful marketers' techniques so can also experience a fantastic ROI!

There's no refuting the truth that when it comes to social media marketing, Facebook is the way to go. Boasting over 2 billion users logging in to Facebook monthly from all corners of the world, it is the king of social media. If you want to advertise to people in your community or on the other side of the world, it's possible to achieve using Facebook ads.

JUST WHAT ARE FACEBOOK ADS?

Anytime you scroll down your Facebook news feed; you'll probably see a post that says "Sponsored" or "Suggested Post" on it. Alternatively, if you're using a desktop computer, you'll see advertisements on the right side of your monitor. You'll even see in-stream video ads while watching videos.

Likewise, you'll see ads or sponsored messages on Facebook Messenger, Instagram, as well as the Audience Network. These are all examples of *Facebook Ads.*

Small businesses, large corporations, and even regular people pay Facebook billions of dollars each year to display their ads to Facebook users. It's not shocking because compared to other platforms, Facebook gives their advertisements the best bang for their buck.

WHY SHOULD YOU ADVERTISE WITH FACEBOOK ADS?

Before I reveal how you can get started with Facebook ads, let me go over a few reasons why you should invest your advertising dollars with this platform.

1. Your prospective customers and clients are all using Facebook.

Okay, maybe not all. However, some, if not most, will have a Facebook account. Of course, not everyone likes Facebook, but anyone who has ever heard of the Internet will know of Facebook. Whether you want to target people in your area or another continent, it's simple to do on Facebook.

2. Hyper-targeting is a Facebook Ads specialty.

When we register for a Facebook account, we provide Facebook with a wide variety of details about ourselves. Advertisers are targeting us with that information. Other ad platforms don't even come close to Facebook ads' targeting options.

You can target people, for example, based on where they live, the hobbies they enjoy, their favorite sports teams, the language they speak, their education, their life status, their profession, their income, their travel preferences, and so much more.

3. Facebook ads won't make you bankrupt.

You won't go bankrupt if, of course, you don't give Facebook all your money. However, doing that wouldn't be a very wise business decision, would it? With Facebook Ads account, you can spend as little as a few dollars each day. Facebook certainly isn't going to complain.

If you compare the amount of money that you'll invest advertising on Google Adwords, Bing ads, native ads, banner ads, billboard or newspaper advertising, you're going to save a lot of money using Facebook Ads! With the amount you'll keep, you'll be able to get to even more of your target market. That is, you can quickly scale your spending and get in front of more people.

4. You can gauge your Facebook Ads performance.

You're not going to be playing the guessing game with Facebook ads. The platform is very transparent and, you can see how many impressions, clicks, and conversions your ads receive in real time. You need to add the Facebook pixel to measure your results.

This snippet of code is all you need to track your website's essential activities – who's buying, who's signed up to your list, who's visited and bounced off your site without doing anything.

5. Advertising on Facebook can also increase traffic on your website and foot traffic into your business.

You can direct people to do whatever you want them to do using Facebook ads. For instance, if you want them to visit your site, include the proper call-to-action within your ad. If you people to visit your physical store, let them know. If you make your ad sufficiently enticing and give people what they want (by addressing their pain points), then you make it easy for them to follow through with your call-to-action.

6. You can quickly get your brand in front of many people.

You can get your ad in front of all 2 billion+ users of Facebook. Not everyone's going to be interested in your brand and what you're selling, though, so can result in high costs. The objective of Facebook ads is to reach the right audience – not just any audience.

When you're targeting the right audience, people will be more open to what you're selling. They will engage more with your ad, which will result in lower ad costs.

7. Facebook ads are more effective than organic Facebook marketing.

Back in the day, you could launch a new Facebook page, and pay a couple of dollars to get people to like your page. Whenever you published an original post, a large percentage of your fans would see your update in their news feeds. It's an entirely different story, today.

With so many people joining, and so many new pages and groups, the Facebook news feed has become crowded. This growth has caused organic reach to drop dramatically. Now, to reach your target audience, it's best to pay Facebook rather than just sitting around waiting for your fans and followers to engage with your latest post.

GETTING STARTED WITH FACEBOOK ADS

There's a steep learning curve that comes with Facebook ads, just like most things in life. Let's take it one step at a time, so you don't get confused and throw money down the drain.

Step 1. Identify Your Objectives

You need to know the objectives you want to accomplish with your advertisements before you start with Facebook. Knowing what you want to achieve with your ads will give you a plan. The point is to set up your ads to meet your goals.

Some example objectives are:

- Get people to like your page.

- Get people to go to your website.

- Get people to sign up for your email list.

- Get people to come to an event.

- Get people to purchase your product.

- Get people to download your latest app.

Identifying your objectives will help you create the most suitable ad for your audience. On Facebook Ads, these are the different goals or campaign objectives you can choose:

(The different campaign objectives available in Facebook Ads)

By looking at the screenshot above, you'll see there are three target categories: **Awareness**, **Consideration**, and **Conversion**.

I'll go over each objective here:

1. **Awareness** – this goal is excellent if you want to connect to cold audiences or people that haven't interacted with your brand or site yet. You can pick between two choices:

a. **Brand Awareness** – you can raise people's awareness of your brand name.

b. **Reach** – you can reach the most significant number of people in your target market choosing this goal.

2. **Consideration** – this objective is superb if you want people to begin thinking of your brand or your company and motivate them to learn more about what you can do for them. You can choose from 6 options:

a. **Traffic** – pick this objective if your desire is for people to visit your website or boost engagement with your app.

b. **App Installs** – if you want people to download and install your mobile app, this is the objective you should select.

c. **Engagement** – if you're going to boost your Facebook posts, promote your Facebook Page, get people to claim an offer on your Page, and get more people to attend an event on your Page, then you need to choose this objective.

d. **Video Views** – to acquire more awareness about your brand, you can produce a video ad that showcases behind the scenes stories or client reviews and endorsements.

e. **Lead Generation** – if you wish to get leads or email addresses from people curious about your business, then use this objective. The Lead Generation objective makes it simple for prospective customers to sign up for your service.

f. **Messages** – get people to send messages to your company using Facebook messenger and even Instagram. This objective will help your business to address questions from prospects, create more leads and deliver more transactions.

3. **Conversion** – conversion ads encourage interested people to purchase your product or sign up for your service. You can choose from three different options:

a. **Conversions** – if you want to send people to your website, Facebook app or mobile app, use this objective. For the best results, track and measure your conversions. You will need to install the Facebook pixel on your site.

b. **Catalog Sales** – to use this objective, you will need to create a catalog to display your inventory. As soon as you have this setup, you can then produce ads that will automatically reveal items from your catalog based on your target audience.

c. **Store Visits** – if you're running a brick-and-mortar business, then you can use this objective to encourage more people to visit and shop at your store.

Step 2. Know Your Audience

- You need to know your audience now that you have set your objectives. Who do you expect your Facebook ads to target?

- Would you like to target women, men, or both?

- Will your product or service be a better fit for single or married people?

- Will 20-30-year-old sports fans be your target market?

- Would you like the attention of people who love classical music in New York?

- Are you going to be selling your products just in the US or will you ship them around the world?

There are more than 2 Billion people that you can target on Facebook right now, as we mentioned before. You merely need to find a specific group of people that your product will benefit the most.

If you don't know your audience, if you're going to target everyone, it can lead to astronomical advertising costs for you. It's best to have an idea who will be most interested in what you have to offer before you start creating your ads.

Developing a customer avatar – your ideal customer – is perfect for this. Not only will you save money, but with the right target audience, you will also get better results.

Step 3. Know Your Budget

Whether your marketing budget is large or small, Facebook ads will help you out. Even if you only have $1 or $2 to spend on ads every day, you can still get your ads in front of a few hundred or a few thousand people. The number of people who see it will, of course, depend on your targeting, ad placement, and overall ad strategy.

At first, expect to lose money while optimizing your ad sets. Every day you can spend $5 on various ads and see which one converts the best. You are going to do a lot of testing.

Trial and error is the name of the game. However, you're going to win big when you find the right combination. Your budget of $5 each day will be a thing of the past.

Starting with Facebook Ads might seem confusing at first, but once you get the hang of the number one social media advertising platform, you're in for an exciting ride!

Read the next chapter to learn more about the Facebook Ads Manager and how to start using it to grow your business.

CHAPTER 2: GETTING FAMILIAR WITH FACEBOOK ADS MANAGER

In this chapter, you will discover exactly how the Facebook Ads Manager works. I'm going to walk you through the different sections and include screenshots to make finding your way around the Ads Manager easier for you.

WHAT IS THE FACEBOOK ADS MANAGER?

For all your Facebook, Instagram, or Audience Network advertisements, the Facebook Ads Manager is your ad campaign command center. Creating new ads, editing and managing your existing ads, viewing your ad reports, managing your Facebook pixel events, billing information, is all handled in your Facebook Ads Manager.

Besides accessing your Ads Manager from a desktop computer, you can also access your ads using the Facebook Ads Manager mobile app. It is available for free download from both the Google Play Store and the Apple App Store. You can use the mobile app to:

- Create new ads

- Track your ads performance

- Edit and manage current ads

- Edit ad budgets and schedules

- Receive push notifications

It's important to mention that you can only handle a single ad account with Ads Manager. You need to create a Facebook Business Manager account if you want to manage more than one ad account. So if you have customers or have to keep your ad accounts separate (such as one ad account for each company or business), then you need the Facebook Business Manager.

HOW TO ACCESS THE FACEBOOK ADS MANAGER

Accessing the Facebook Ads Manager is simple. Follow the steps below:

Step 1. Log in to your account on Facebook

Step 2. On the top navigation bar, you will see the white triangular arrow. Click this **arrow,** then click **Create Ads** (see image below).

Business Manager:

    Create Page

    Manage Pages

    Create Group

    New Groups   20+

    Create Ads

    Manage Ads

    Activity log   20+

    News Feed Preferences

    Settings

    Log out

Step 3. Your Ad Manager will be set up by Facebook. You're going to see this on your screen while you're waiting. Don't worry; it will only take a moment.

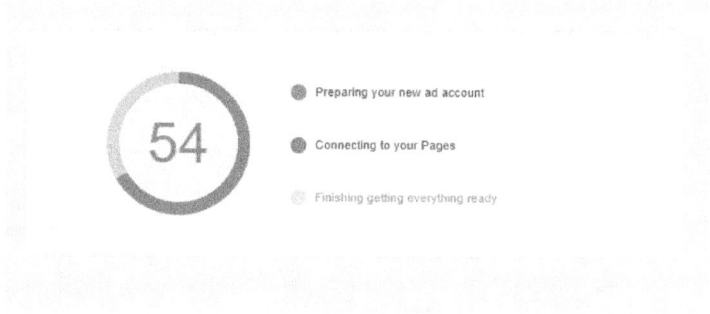

Step 4. When you finish setting up your Ads Manager on Facebook, something like this will appear on your screen:

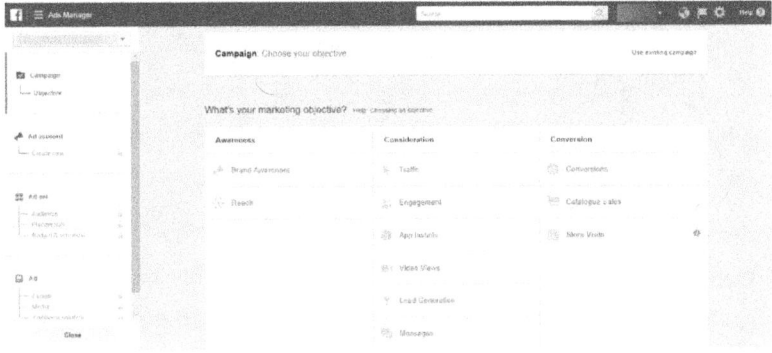

Now that you understand how to access the Ads Manager for Facebook let me show you how to create your first Facebook ad.

HOW TO CREATE AN ADVERTISEMENTISEMENT USING THE FACEBOOK ADS MANAGER

Just follow the steps I outlined in the previous section to access the Facebook Ads Manager when you are ready to create an ad. You must go through 3 different levels in the Ads Manager – the **campaign** level, the **ad set** level, and the **ad** level.

Level 1 - Campaign Level

In Chapter 1, I mentioned that before setting up your Facebook ads, you should have an advertising objective in mind. Keep this objective in mind when choosing from any of the 11 goals below and determine the most appropriate goal from the list:

1. Brand awareness
2. Reach

3. Traffic

4. Engagement

5. App installs

6. Video views

7. Lead generation

8. Messages

9. Conversions

10. Catalog sales

11. Store visits

Once you have selected your marketing objective, your campaign name will be your objective. I chose the Traffic goal in this example; therefore, my name of the campaign is Traffic. You can edit the name of the campaign as you see fit.

You can edit your budget at the Campaign Level as you can see near the bottom of the above screenshot.

Click the blue *Set up ad account* button when you are ready to proceed. Then you will be sent to this page:

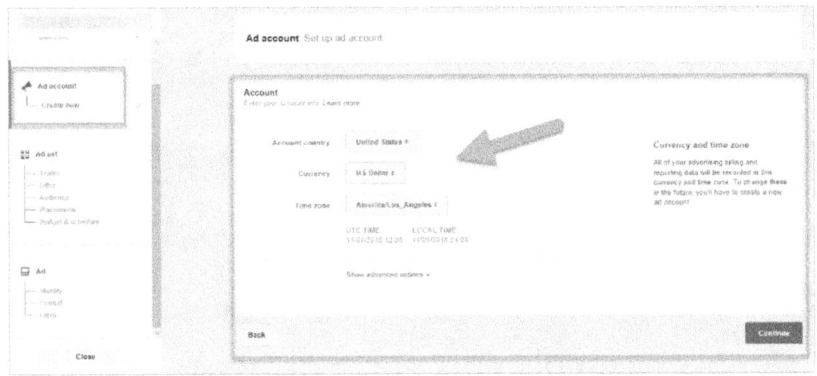

Setting up your ad account is straightforward. From the list, select your **country**, then your **currency**, and finally, your **time zone**. Click **Continue**. We're going to the second level now.

Level 2 – Ad Set Level

The options that will appear in the Ad Set level will depend on your chosen goal. If you want, you can always go back to the Campaign level and change the goal so you can see the various options. The three options present in the ALL campaigns Ad Set level are as follows:

- Audience

- Placements

- Budget & schedule

In this chapter, I'm going to **Traffic** as my campaign objective. These are the options available for Traffic campaigns at the Ad Set level:

You should fill out the various sections at this point with information relevant to your particular campaign. If you use a Traffic campaign like I am in this example, here is more information about the different settings you need to define at the Ad Set level:

- Traffic–choose if you want people to go to your website, app or send a message to Messenger

- Offer – You can create an offer that people can save and receive reminders about if you run a promotion in your business.

- Audience – this is where you define to whom you want to show your ads. You can create a new audience, use a saved audience, or create a custom audience made up of people who have had any interaction with your business.

- Placements – you can choose to have Facebook select the placements automatically or choose yourself manually. Manual placement gives you the most control over your ads. It's best to select manual placements so you can decide if you want to display your ads on desktop computers, mobile devices, right-hand column, Instagram, Audience Network, or Messenger.

- Budget and schedule – You can choose whether to use a daily budget or a lifetime budget in this section. Facebook will give you your weekly ad spend estimate.

Level 3 – Ad Level

The Ad level options you see will depend on the goal of your Campaign. You will notice different options at the Ad Level if you choose Brand Awareness as your goal. If you select Conversions, you will see an entirely different set of options.

Since in this chapter we have chosen Traffic as our ad target, these are the options available at the Ad level:

You will have to specify the following details for the Traffic campaign Ad level:

- **Identity** – Select your Facebook page or Instagram account.

- **Format** – Decide how to look at your ad. You can choose from Carousel, Single Image, Single Video, Slideshow or Collection ad formats as you can see in the screenshot. If you selected mobile placements at the Ad Set level, you could even add a full-screen landing page to your ad for a more immersive experience for those who engaged with your ad.

- **Links** – This is where the text, images or videos for your ad are written down. You can also view the preview of your ad here so that you can see what your ad looks like based on the ad placements you have chosen at the Ad Set level.

With the various settings, you can play around until you are happy with how your advertisement looks. Hit the green Confirm button when you are ready to publish.

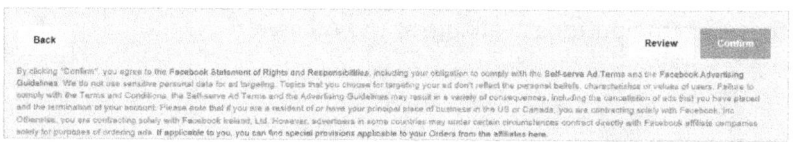

A QUICK TOUR OF THE TOOLS AVAILABLE ON THE FACEBOOK ADS MANAGER

Click Ads Manager at the top left corner to access all the tools on your Ads Manager. Then, as you see below, you will see the Ads Manager menu. If you don't see the same picture, click on All Tools at the bottom:

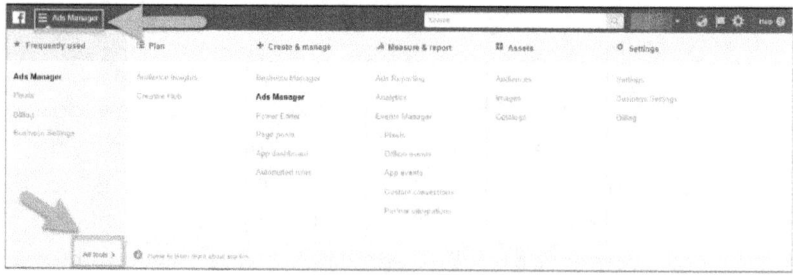

The Ads Manager menu is divided into six columns, as you can see in the screenshot.

1. **Frequently Used column** —contains a link to 4 of your most commonly used tools in the Ads Manager

2. **Plan column** – this column gives you access to **Audience Insights** and **Creative Hub**

- **Audience Insights** – this is where you build hyper-targeted audiences. You can play with a variety of data on Facebook and target people based on their location, interests, and behaviors.

- **Creative Hub** – If you're not prepared to pay for real ads, but want to see how it looks like to your audience, go to Creative Hub and create your ads mockups. You can also check the percentage of text in the images you will be using in your advertisements. If your image contains too much text, the ad's reach may be affected.

3. **Create & Manage** – in this column; you have access to six different tools, such as:

   - **Business Manager** – this is just a link to the Facebook Business is where you manage several ad accounts in a single location

   - **Ads Manager** – this is where you develop your Facebook ads (in the previous section of this chapter I gave an overview of how to create ads)

   - **Power Editor** – you can import and export ads and edit your work in the Power Editor

   - **Page posts** – new posts can be created here. By going to your page, you can also create posts. You can choose to use your newly created post as an ad in this menu or have it published on your page as well.

- **App dashboard** – you can create and manage settings for your apps in your app dashboard if you are a Facebook app developer

- **Automated rules** – you've got more control on your hands with automated rules. You don't have to check your campaigns every day. Simply set up automated rules that will notify or update you if there are changes in your campaigns, ad sets, or ads.

4. **Measure & Report column** – You can track and measure your ads and events in this column. This column's tools are:

- **Ads Reporting** – to view your most important ad metrics, you can create and export Ads Manager reports. Additionally, you can schedule reports to be sent directly to you by email.

- **Analytics** – this tool will help you to analyze your Facebook pages and the pixels installed on your website.

- **Events Manager** – You can create and manage your Facebook pixels, offline events, app events, add custom conversions and partner integrations with this tool.

5. **Assets column** – You can easily access essential assets that you used or will use to create your ads in this section, including:

- **Audiences** – This tool helps you create and manage custom audiences, lookalike audiences, and saved audiences

- **Images** – you can upload and manage images for your pages and ads using this tool

- **Catalogs** – You can add and manage your inventory here if you have a store with many products.

6. **Settings column** - In this column, you can access three tools. They are:

   - **Settings** – Access your ad account settings, payment settings, your pages, email, and Facebook notifications here.

   - **Business settings** – If you've set up a Business Manager, you'll be managing your ad accounts, pages, and anyone who works on them.

   - **Billing** –manage your payment settings here, and you can see all the transactions in your ad account that have ever occurred

NEED HELP GETTING AROUND YOUR FACEBOOK ADS MANAGER?

There's no reason to be afraid of getting lost in the Ads Manager maze. Type your query on the **search bar** if you need help with anything. Alternatively, in the upper right corner of your screen, you can click the Help button, and the **Advertiser Help Center** will appear on your screen.

Here's where you find these useful tools:

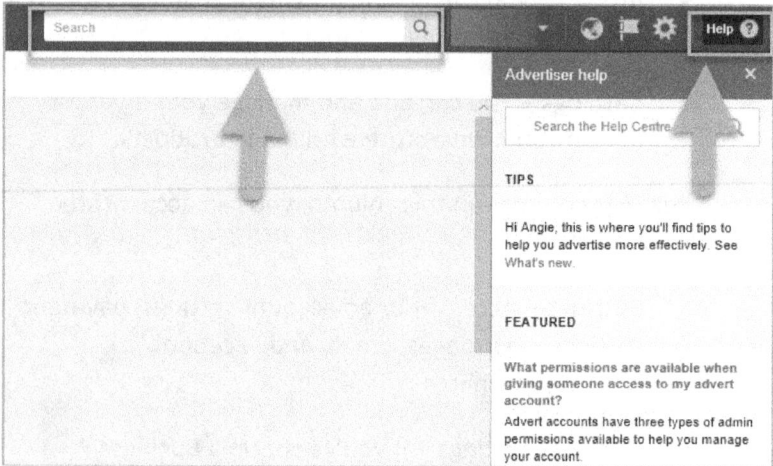

FINAL THOUGHTS ON THE ADS MANAGER

I hope this chapter helped you learn more about the Facebook Ads Manager and how to start creating your first Facebook ad. Let's move on to compare and contrast Facebook Ads and Boosted Posts.

CHAPTER 3: FACEBOOK ADS VERSUS BOOSTED POSTS

The first two chapters covered Facebook Ads and the Facebook Ads Manager in detail. I discussed how and why you need to get started with Facebook Ads.

There are numerous advantages to producing an ad using the Ads Manager. However, it does have a steep learning curve connected to it if you would like to know a faster and less complicated method to get your very first ad released. After that, you need to think about boosting a post.

In this chapter, we will compare and contrast Facebook Ads and Boosted Posts so you can choose which approach is best for your business objectives. But first, I'll cover Boosted Posts and show you exactly how they work.

Now, I assume you already have a Facebook page set up for your business. If you don't have one yet, make an effort to create one now. You can always modify your page settings later.

Let's get started!

WHAT ARE FACEBOOK BOOSTED POSTS?

If you're an administrator of the Facebook page, you won't miss the Blue **Boost Post** button that appears on your page in every post. If you don't see that button on your timeline anywhere, you probably aren't a page admin. Make sure that you are one so that you can follow in this chapter the steps I have written down.

Boosted posts are posts that are published on your Facebook page to *boost* or promote your followers or other target audience. Your posts appear on the timeline of your page, so if someone visits your page, they can see all of your posts, both boosted and unboosted.

If you're asking why you need to boost a post to people who already like your page, then read on for the explanation.

A few years back, posts published on a fan page were immediately seen by the people who liked and followed that page. This lead to a lot of free organic traffic and engagement levels were through the roof (think 80-90% of fans engaging with every post!). However, over recent years, organic reach has been on a steady decline.

Several page owners are reporting that their organic engagement has dropped to 1-5% per post! Essentially this implies that if you have 10,000 followers, only a few hundred people will see your post. If that number is a few million followers, only a few thousand people will ever see your post and engage with it.

The drop in follower engagement is why page likes are generally a vanity metric nowadays. It looks great on your page but if only a tiny percentage of your fans see your posts. So why bother buying page likes? If you want to increase the possibility of your followers seeing your all-important post, then you need to think about boosting your post instead.

HOW TO BOOST A FACEBOOK POST

First, you'll need to head to your Facebook page. After that look for the post, you wish to boost. Find the blue button at the bottom right corner of your post that says **Boost Post** and click it.

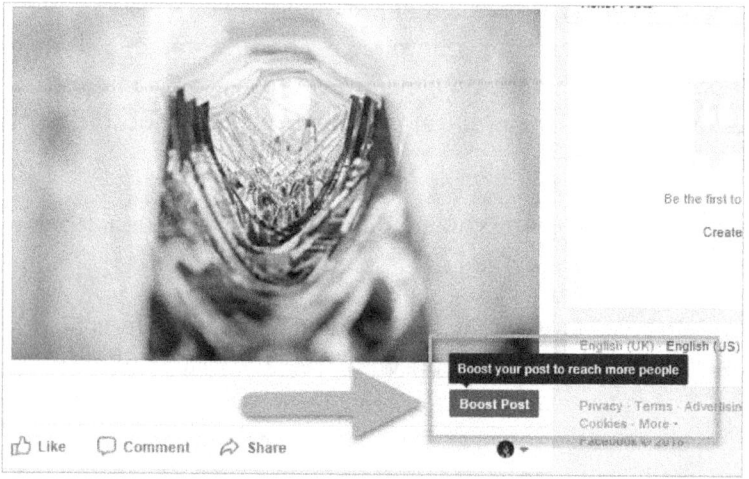

Unlike the seemingly complex Facebook Ads Manager user interface that I shared in Chapter 2, the Boost Post interface is reasonably simple and straightforward:

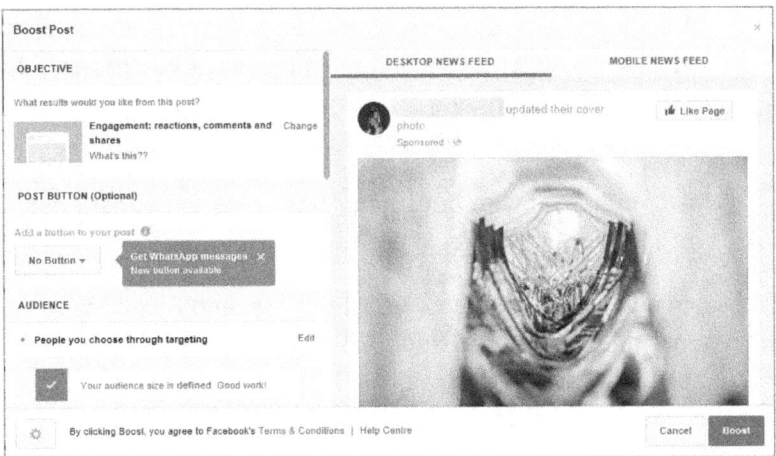

When boosting a post, you have fewer choices to select from unlike with Facebook Ads. Here is a list of the options you can change:

1. **Objective** – you can choose if you like to get more **engagement** (responses, comments, shares), get people to **visit your website**, or **receive messages** from your target audience.

2. **Call to action button** – you can pick to have no button, or you can utilize Shop Now, Learn More, Sign Up, Book Now, Send Message, or Send WhatsApp Message.

3. **Audience** – you can select people through targeting, people who like your page, and people who like your page plus their friends.

4. **Budget and Duration** – you can choose your daily budget for the period of your campaign. The minimum daily budget is $1.

5. **Tracking conversions** – you can make use of the Facebook pixel to track your conversions. To use this feature, you need to have the pixel installed on your website.

6. **Payment** – you can specify the currency you'd like to use for your payment here and the ad account you're going to be paying from (you will have several options if you link your Facebook page to your Business Manager)

When you're ready to boost your post, click the **Boost Post** button and Facebook will begin promoting your post.

Since you understand how Boosted Posts and Facebook Ads work (remember Chapters 1 and 2), it's time to compare them, so you're able an informed decision when the time comes for you to do some Facebook content promotion.

MAIN DISTINCTIONS BETWEEN BOOSTED POSTS AND FACEBOOK ADS

Whether you're in the Boosted Posts camp or a firm believer in Facebook Ads, they both have their advantages and benefits. We will look at critical features in this section.

1. **Campaign Objective**

    - Boosted posts - select between three objectives (*engagement, traffic, messages*)

    - Ads - choose as many as 11 campaign goals (*brand awareness, reach, video views, lead generation, traffic, engagement, app installs, messages, conversions, catalog sales, and store visits*).

2. **Budget Control**

- Boosted posts – you only get to choose your total budget

- Ads – you can select either your daily or lifetime budget

3. **Ad Scheduling**

   - Boosted posts – when you boost your post, it will begin immediately. You aren't able to schedule it, but you can set an end date.

   - Ads - you can establish a start and end date for your ads so if you're going to be unavailable, you can plan your ads in advance and they can run even while you're away.

4. **Audience Targeting**

   - Boosted posts – you can choose audience targeting; however, it's minimal. For example, you can't target people by their language, and you can't add a connection type. You can target people who liked your page as well as their friends.

   - Ads – you can hyper-target your audience using Facebook ads. You can use custom audiences, lookalike audiences, target by language; you can even include connection types. There's also an option to let Facebook automatically broaden your interests if it believes people outside of your target audience will engage with your advertisement.

5. **Geographic Targeting** – you can target specific places with both boosted posts and advertisements.

6. **Age and Gender Targeting** – you can include the age and gender of your target audience with both boosted posts and ads.

7. **Interest and Behavior Targeting** - you can choose to target your audience's interests and behaviors with both boosted posts and advertisements.

8. **Language Targeting**

    - Boosted posts – you cannot target your audience's language

    - Ads – with ads you can target language

9. **Ad Placement**

    - Boosted posts – posts only appear on desktop and mobile news feeds. You can't select only "desktop" or only "mobile."

    - Ads – you have complete control over where you want your ads to show up. You can choose to have them appear just on desktop news feeds, or only on mobile news feeds, column, instant articles, Instagram, audience network, and more.

10. **Dark Post**

    - Boosted post – you cannot create a dark post with boosted posts. A boosted post must be published and will be present on your page's timeline.

    - Ads –you can create a post specifically for ad use, and you can select not to have it displayed on your page timeline

11. **Ad Delivery**

   - Boosted post – you can't change how your ads are delivered

   - Ads – you can pick between *standard* and *accelerated* delivery. You need to set a bid cap to use accelerated delivery which is works for time-sensitive promotions.

12. **Instagram Ads**

   - Boosted post – you aren't able to boost your Facebook post on Instagram

   - Ads – yes, you can choose to display your ads by ticking "Instagram" in the Placements section

13. **Audience Network Ads**

   - Boosted post – you can't boost your Facebook post on the Audience Network

   - Ads – you can opt to present your ads in the Audience Network by ticking it in the Placements section

14. **Right Column Ads**

   - Boosted post – you cannot display your boosted post in the right column on desktop computers

   - Ads – you can select to show your ads in the right column on desktop computers.

15. **Retargeting**

   - Boosted post – you are not able to retarget people

   - Ads – yes, you need to ensure the Facebook pixel is installed on your website and is working correctly

THE RIGHT TIME TO USE BOOSTED POSTS
INSTEAD OF ADS

There are several benefits to using Facebook Ads, but in certain situations, Boosted Posts will perform just as well, and at a much quicker rate. Consider using Boosted Posts:

1. If you have a post that's already getting excellent organic engagement, then you might consider boosting it. If the people who viewed your post organically are engaging with it, that is, they're liking, sharing and commenting on it, it's likely that those who did not see your post in their news feeds will also find it interesting.

2. If your post is informative, that is, you're not trying to sell anything, then people might be more receptive to your boosted post. If you're selling something, then it's better to use Facebook Ads since you have more formatting options.

3. If you have time constraints and you don't want to learn the intricacies of Facebook Ads Manager, then boosting a post is the better option.

With that said, boosting posts is, basically, for newbies. If you want more value, then you need to dive in and learn how the Facebook Ads Manager works.

WHEN YOU SHOULD USE FACEBOOK ADS INSTEAD OF BOOSTED POSTS

In general, Facebook Ads are a significantly better choice than Boosted Posts merely because it provides advertisers complete control over their ads.

The Ads Manager will let you split test every single facet of your ad campaign. It's so much more versatile, and in the long run, your campaign will be much more lucrative.

You can hyper-target your audience and reach even more people with the same qualities as your winning audience (you do this by making a lookalike audience – something you aren't able to do on boosted posts).

Creating custom audiences is simple and thanks to the audience insight tool you can discover the best demographics for who might be the best fit for your offer.

With Facebook Ads, you have several different types of campaign objectives from which to pick. With Boosted Posts, you can only choose from a few options. Since you're investing money into your marketing, either way, it's best to dive in and use Facebook Ads.

If you think it's beyond your ability level or it's too technical, you can always work with an agency or a consultant to give you a hand with your Facebook Ads campaign. My contact information is at the back of the book.

FINAL WORDS

Boosted Posts work fantastic on its own and is great for beginners who are just beginning with paid promotion. But, it gives you minimal control over your ads and may not be the most economical choice for your business.

If you want full control over exactly how your ads run and identify the best possible ads that will convert with your target audience, then you need Facebook Ads. Granted, figuring out how to manage Facebook Ads is not the most straightforward job but it will be worth it in the long-run particularly after you discover the right combination of high-converting ads and target audience.

While Facebook Ads and Boosted Posts are excellent promotion methods, there are still numerous other things to consider. In the next chapter, we will discuss optimizing your Facebook Ad design – because first impressions make a difference, especially to cold audiences.

CHAPTER 4: HOW TO OPTIMIZE YOUR FACEBOOK AD DESIGN

We discussed the technical aspects of Facebook Ads in the previous chapters. We'll discuss how to optimize your Facebook ad design in this chapter because if you don't, you may just as well flush your money down the drain.

Try not to get lost in the technical elements of your ad design because it is just as important to design your ad and to make sure that your target audience notices it.

WHY OPTIMIZE YOUR FACEBOOK AD DESIGN?

I'd like you to consider the last time you scrolled through Facebook before I answer this question. In what cases have you stopped scrolling to see an ad that appeared on your feed?

Was it due to the name of the Page? Or was the picture they used eye-catching? Or did the headline somehow attract your attention? Or maybe they used a video that told the story of the brand?

Whatever it was, it worked well enough to stop scrolling through your news feed. The people behind the ad surely considered how they could get people like you to take notice of their ad as part of their target market. They ensured that their ad layout would be optimized so that their ad would not go unnoticed and ignored.

This example is only one of the possible answers to the above question. Here are a few more reasons why your Facebook ad design should be optimized:

1. **Great ad design makes your target market connect with your brand**. You need to optimize your Facebook ad design so you can engage people in your target market with your ad and do whatever you want them to do so that you can meet your campaign goal. If you want them to download a free eBook, this should be encouraged by your ad design, and you should get people to download it.

2. **Your design communicates your brand**. If your design looks elegant and luxurious, your brand will be associated with being an elegant and luxurious brand. If your design is fun, you'll be considered by people as a fun-loving brand.

3. **Good design makes you more visible to people**. If you've ever found a unique ad that's been viral or shared by many, many people, you can understand why good design makes your brand highly visible. The more unique your ad design is, the more people are going to share your ad. Remember that getting excellent organic reach to a paid ad helps to reduce your ad costs.

4. **Good design drives conversions**. Don't underestimate the power of good design at any time. When you have a well-designed, compelling advertisement, it speaks directly to people who see your ad. They will be more willing to follow your call-to-action if they see themselves in your design.

For example, if you were a grandmother and you see an ad with a warm-hearted picture of a child hugging his grandma, wouldn't you be compelled to follow the call-to-action of the ad? Wouldn't you click on the Buy Now button to buy that sweater for your grandkid if the ad was selling a child's handmade sweater?

5. **Good design reinforces your ad's message**.
Understanding what this point means is essential. Some advertisers are only concerned with having a nice picture in their ad. Some just care about the message because they think it's more important than their ad graphics. An advertisement using an eye-catching image AND conveys a message that resonates with the target will result in more conversions. In advertising, continuity is crucial. If you complement each other with your message and image, you will have the recipe for success.

Now that you know why it is critical to optimize your ad let's discuss how you can optimize your Facebook ad design.

HOW TO OPTIMIZE YOUR FACEBOOK AD DESIGN

If you want to optimize your Facebook ad design, there are many factors you need to consider. As previously mentioned, your message and your accompanying graphic should complement each other. Psychology also plays a significant role in design so we'll go over that here.

1) Use Great Visuals

When you use captivating and attractive visuals or graphics, people are more likely to stop scrolling through their news feed to take a better look at your ad. If you use dull or uninspired images that don't stand out in people's crowded news feeds, and expect NOT to get a lot of interaction with your ad.

Additionally, it's essential to keep in mind that Facebook does not like too much text on images. Whenever you upload images for your ad, the Facebook algorithm will inspect the images for text. Having excessive text will impact the delivery of your ad so ensure you pass this requirement.

Here are a few tips to make sure you use the right visuals for your ad:

- **Use high-quality images** - Some stock images are excellent; however, most of them are used excessively. If you have original images that show off your brand and your customers, then you should use them. People love authentic and original images; stock graphics often look phony, and the majority of smart Facebook users can pick out tacky stock images immediately. The majority will most likely skip your advertisement and keep scrolling down their news feeds.

- **Use original graphics** – This choice is a little bit costly; however, if you want to stand apart, you can work with a graphic designer to produce original graphics for your advertisement. By doing this, you know your ad will be distinct and may raise the likelihood of people engaging and sharing your advertisement with their friends.

- **Use close-up photos of people's faces** –

    If you're promoting a more melancholy occasion, however, then you must use the right imagery. You probably don't want to use a joyful picture if you're advertising something like a funeral home (however this depends on your target market and how you position your ad).

- **Use location-specific images** – If you are advertising a local business, you should consider using graphics that highlight your city or state. As an example, if you're promoting a company in San Antonio, Texas, you can probably use a picture with the Alamo as a backdrop. People who recognize the Alamo will know your ad relates to San Antonio or Texas.

- **Use visual contrast or filters** – Using the ideal contrast and filter for your photos are very beneficial. There's a reason that filters on Instagram are so prominent – people love using them. Be sure that you don't overuse them though. Too much filter and contrast may communicate the wrong message to your target market – and that message is they see an ad created by an amateur.

- **Use carousel ads if possible** - Carousel ads are remarkable if you have exceptional and high-grade photos. You can produce a motif or a story with just a few linked pictures, and carousel ads are excellent for this purpose. When used appropriately, carousel ads create an impact comparable to a panoramic shot. Look at this great example from Facebook. Wouldn't you say it's captivating?

(Four images in a carousel ad made to look like a panorama. Source: Facebook.com)

2) Have An Excellent Value Proposition

Now that you've caught the interest of your target market thanks to the excellent graphics you've used in your advertisement, they'll wonder what you're offering them.

Here is where the value of your proposition comes in. You have to convince your viewers that picking your brand over your competitors will give them outstanding value.

For example, if you're promoting a health club membership, it should be clear in your ad that you're providing something of really high value for a fraction of the normal cost. You can say that for the first 100 clients who take you up on your offer, they're going to get a discount of 80% off their club membership.

Who wouldn't love that?

You can list what is included with your membership in your advertisement so that they can make an immediate decision that your offer is too good to pass. Let's not forget the scarcity shown in the ad. Telling the ad viewers the deal will encourage the first 100 people to act.

So where do you find your incredible value proposition? Of course, it will be in the headline and your advertisement summary. This is why you need to be sure that the headline captures the attention of your reader when writing your ad copy.

WRITE A GREAT HEADLINE THAT HIGHLIGHTS YOUR INCREDIBLE OFFER:

- **Mention the pain point you're solving** – If you're solving an issue, mention it in the headline. Do not make your target market search for it in the ad copy. People only take a few seconds for your ad – maximize it by telling them what they want to read!

- **Ask questions** – The natural response of people when you ask a question in your headline is to answer it in their minds. Some people may reject it, but most of the time people will stop scrolling long enough to answer your question in their minds if you ask the right type of question.

- **Add a little humor** – A funny and amusing headline is catchy, for sure. A headline that gets a response from your target audience is a great advertising tool so try to think of something funny that will bring a smile to your readers face, even for just a second.

- **Use language your audience will understand** – If you're targeting a particular group of people, understand their language. If you're going after fishing enthusiasts, you may want to use some references to fishing. Generally, try to get your audience's interest and their trust by showing them that you speak their language.

Once you've nailed down your headline, you can put the rest of the information in your ad copy. Keep your description short and concise. People don't want to read an essay – it will turn them off from your brand – and they'll keep scrolling through their news feed.

Include social evidence and user testimonials in your ad copy. Select the best ones if you have customer reviews and include them in your advertisement. If you have multiple users or clients, mention that as well.

3) Have A Clear Call-To-Action

Even if you have the most eye-catching graphics used in your advertisement and the most appealing headline ever created, if your call-to-action isn't clear people are will be confused by what you want them to do.

If you plan to get conversions, then you need a clear call-to-action on your ad. You're paying Facebook for your advertisements; consequently you want to ensure you're getting the most out of your investment.

For example, if you want people to download a PDF, make it clear in your ad that you will give them access to a PDF that will fix some pain point for them. If you want to sell something from your store, make it easy for them to do so.

FINAL WORDS

Maximizing your ad design for Facebook is an integral part of your ad campaign. You can have a highly effective Facebook ad campaign with the appropriate target market and the ideal ad design.

In the next chapter, I will reveal how using custom targeted audiences your advertisement can gain maximum exposure. So, let's move on.

CHAPTER 5: MAXIMIZE YOUR EXPOSURE WITH CUSTOM TARGETED AUDIENCES

In this chapter, you will learn everything about custom audiences and lookalike audiences. You will discover how you can target these two audiences to get optimal exposure on Facebook. To start, let's define the terms: *custom audiences* and *lookalike audiences*.

WHAT IS A CUSTOM AUDIENCE?

A custom audience on Facebook consists of a group of people who interact on Facebook or other platforms and even offline with your business. Because these people already know your brand, it usually leads to **higher conversions** to target such a group. For your business, they are not strangers. They are what we call an audience 'warm' or 'hot.'

The target market you create at the **Ad Set** level (we'll call this the default targeting system) can be targeted using their location, age, languages, interests, gender, connections, and more.

While this default targeting system is extremely detailed on its own, the **Custom Audience** feature gives advertisers the ability to reach people you can't target with the standard settings you find in the **Audience** tab in **Ads Manager**.

THE 5 TYPES OF CUSTOM AUDIENCES YOU CAN BUILD ON FACEBOOK

Here is a screenshot of the various types of custom audiences you can target with Facebook ads:

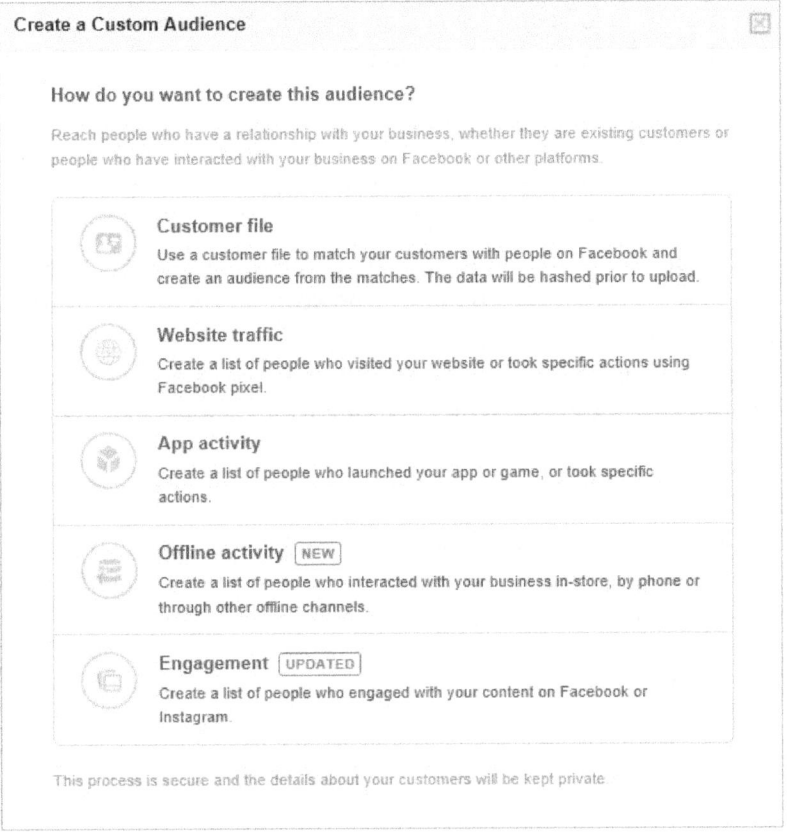

(The different types of custom audiences you can target with Facebook ads)

1. Customer file

If you gather email address from your blog subscribers, you have an email list. You can upload your list to Facebook, and it will search for your subscribers' Facebook accounts. Their email addresses can also be imported directly from MailChimp.

If you don't have an email list, but you have a file of your subscribers that include any of the following information – *email address, phone number, name, Facebook user ID, date of birth, gender, age, city, zip code, and more* –Facebook can use this information to look up your customers' Facebook accounts and include them in your custom audience.

2. Website traffic

You need to install the Facebook pixel on your site to develop an audience from people who have visited and taken specific actions on your website. It's not complicated to install the pixel. To ensure that there are no errors, however, ask someone who knows how to install the pixel for assistance. Also, wait at least 30 days for useful data to get Facebook to read more accurately and create a larger audience size for your custom audience.

3. App activity

If you have an app or game connected to your account, you can create a custom audience of people on your app or game who have started or taken specific actions.

4. Offline activity

You can target people who have interacted in-store, by telephone or other offline.

5. Engagement

The engagement option enables you to target people who have engaged with your content either on Facebook or Instagram. Engagement consists of people who have viewed your videos, opened or completed one of your lead forms, opened your collection or canvas advertisements and interacted with your events.

Facebook ensures that the process is secure in any of the above custom audience options and that information about your customers is kept private. In other words, you won't be able to see your custom audience's individual profiles.

WHAT IS A LOOKALIKE AUDIENCE?

A lookalike audience is one that has similar attributes to another existing audience. Facebook has an active user-base of about 2 billion people that logs onto each month. The Facebook algorithm is so advanced it can detect and identify people who resemble your first group.

The algorithm will look for patterns and qualities that your first group has in common and will create a second group of very similar users that were most likely not previously connected to your business.

You can create a lookalike audience based on a customer list, your Facebook conversion pixel, a custom audience, or people who like your page.

As an example, if you have a custom audience of 20-25-year-old single females based in the Canada who like hockey, you can create a lookalike of that audience by targeting the same demographic of women in the United States or Finland or wherever else you want.

Here's a screenshot of the information required to build a lookalike audience:

Facebook does the hard work for you. All you need to do is pick the audience source, the new location, the number of lookalike audiences you want to create and choose the audience size. That's all there is to it – wait a little while, and you'll have your lookalike audience!

HOW TO USE CUSTOM AND LOOKALIKE AUDIENCES TO GET MORE CONVERSIONS

There are a variety of approaches that you can use for your business to get more conversions. However, using a combination of custom and lookalike audiences is the fastest way to get more sales and leads.

Custom audiences are people who already know about your brand, as we discussed earlier in this chapter. They may already like you and trust you, and would, therefore, be more willing to sign up or purchase your products and services.

Here are a few methods to try using to get more lead conversions for your business:

1. Get In Touch With Old Customers

If your business is new to Facebook and you want to gain more social proof by having people like your Facebook page who know your business, you can try to set up a campaign targeting everyone who has ever done business with you. You can upload your mailing list, subscriber or customer database, and your Facebook profiles will match your information.

You can start an engagement campaign when you set up your custom audience and have your current customers like your page. Be sure to clearly identify who you are in your advertisement so that they can recognize you.

It's crucial to keep in mind that most marketers consider Page Likes a vanity metric nowadays. Organic engagement from page fans and followers are amazingly low; however, having a 'warm' audience liking your page is advantageous for a couple of reasons:

- The numbers look great on your page (once again, this is a vanity metric), and

- It equates to lower conversion costs.

Facebook professionals agree that it seems to be a common trend to have lower conversion costs when targeting a page's fans. Yes, you still need to pay Facebook to connect with all your fans, but it's not going to break the bank (results may vary from page to page so approach this advice with cautiously).

The reason this method typically leads to lower conversion costs is that' warm' page fans are more likely to click through or engage with your ads as they already know, like, and trust you.

You can create a second advertisement after you've racked up a good number of page likes offering them a sweet deal— something like a loyalty discount for returning customers.

People love discounts! If they've had a positive experience with your business in the past, the chances are good that they'll take you up on your offer.

When you see excellent results on this preliminary campaign, you can then develop a lookalike audience and target a lot more people with the same attributes as your original custom audience!

Remember that's just one of several approaches. You can even get rid of the Page Likes campaign and go straight with the loyalty offer to target your custom audience. It's up to you—and your budget!

2. Offer New or Upgraded Products to Existing Customers

In this approach, customer segmentation plays a significant role. Simply put, you would have to create one list for each product if you sell several products. Yes, it will take a lot of upfront work, but when it's time to create those ads, it's going to make your job much easier.

Here's an example:

Say you're offering ten products (A to J products). Keep a list of all the customers who purchased each product for each product you sell. In a few months, you're going to release an updated version of, say Product A 2.0. It's not a completely new product, but it has significant upgrades to version 1.0.

If you offer version 2.0 at $100, you can set up a Facebook ad campaign to target those who purchased version 1.0 and offer a deep discount on the new version (for example, a 50% discount).

Next, you set up a separate advertisement targeting those who did not buy Product A, but bought products B to J and offer Product A 2.0 at the original $100 price (or maybe give them a small discount for being a past customer).

The key to this is that the more specific your audience is, the more ads you can create that speak to them directly and address their pain points. Not only will it lead to fewer people engaging with your ad, but it will also lead to higher conversion costs. The more specific your audience is the more engaged they are, and the lower the cost of your conversion.

Create a lookalike audience for every custom audience to get even more conversions. That means you create 10 Lookalike Audiences if you have ten custom audiences based on each product (Products A to J). This strategy is particularly useful when your products are focused on different markets or industries.

3. Target Subscribers Who Never Read Your Emails

People are continually getting many emails from marketers and companies. We hear marketers say this common expression all the time – "*the money is in the list.*" But if people are getting inundated with emails every single day, the chances that your emails (and everyone not on their contact list) go into the Spam folder or some other folder they will never open.

However, with Facebook Ads, you have a new channel to reach them. You can upload your email list and produce an ad targeted especially to your subscribers.

Offer them something tempting or perhaps just let them know about your new blog post and how valuable it can be. To get your brand in front of them, you need to be creative so that they will remember you when they need your products or services.

True, the money is still "in the list" – you only have to pay a little more for Facebook so you can reach those who choose to ignore your emails.

A WORD OF ADVICE ON CUSTOM AUDIENCES

I hope you can see just how powerful custom audiences and lookalike audiences are. But don't be trigger happy. Don't think you can use stolen Facebook data – or purchased lists – and target people who have never signed up to your list. You can get into a lot of trouble with Facebook if you do this, and you may get your account banned!

Before you create any custom audience, you'd need to ensure the following:

1. You have approval from your customers or subscriber list to use their information. In other words, don't build a custom audience using data you've bought from third-party, unscrupulous marketers. Third-party lists fundamentally go against the premise of custom audiences, which are people who have interacted with your business in the past.

2. The people included in your custom audience have not opted out or unsubscribed from your email list. If people have opted out of your list, it means that they don't want more communication from you. They aren't interested in receiving your emails, your newsletters, and they don't want to see your Facebook advertisements.

If you don't follow these rules, your ad account may be banned. If your target audience lives and breathes on Facebook, getting banned is probably one of the worst things that can happen to any business. So make sure that when targeting custom audiences you don't go against the rules!

CHAPTER 6: HOW TO USE RETARGET MARKETING WITH FACEBOOK

I'm quite sure that in this day and age, you've been retargeted or remarketed by numerous marketers on Facebook. Picture this scenario: you're looking at luxury watches on a random website, and a couple of minutes later you log into Facebook.

While browsing through your news feed, you see an advertisement for the luxury watches you found earlier. Do you think it's a strange coincidence or some Voodoo magic? It's not. That's Facebook retarget marketing at work, and it's what we're going to be discussing in depth in this chapter.

THE ROLE OF FACEBOOK'S PIXEL IN RETARGET MARKETING

Initially, you need to place the Facebook Pixel on your site to set up a retarget marketing campaign and reap practically unlimited opportunities for your business. If you don't have a website, you can't launch a retargeting campaign. Of course, we can help you with getting a website built at https://focusedidea.com.

If this sounds too technical for you, don't fret, you can easily hire a web developer or designer to create your website and have your Facebook pixel installed on it.

EXACTLY WHAT IS THE FACEBOOK PIXEL?

The Facebook pixel is a piece of code you need to insert into the heading of your website. It's only a few lines of code, but it can add a great deal to the bottom-line of your business!

Returning to the scenario, we described at the start of this chapter, here's what took place:

That website had the pixel of Facebook installed, and when you went to visit their website, it left a cookie (not a real cookie, mind you, but a small piece of code) on your browser that enabled the website to track your actions on their site.

If the website owners set up a pixel to track particular events like clicking a button or visiting a specific page, they can also follow if you do any of these tagged events.

They probably tagged you as somebody who visited the site but didn't buy anything in your specific case and added you to their custom audience for retargeting later on Facebook. Therefore, you've seen the luxury watch ad.

WHY YOU SHOULD SET UP THE PIXEL IMMEDIATELY

The Facebook pixel is so powerful that even if you don't have any immediate advertising plans on Facebook, experts suggest you set it up. Setting it up enables your pixel to collect data from your site visitors so you can incorporate your pixel data to your custom audience when you are finally ready to pay for ads.

Just as we covered in the previous chapter, it's much easier to target a custom audience (or people who have engaged with your business before) than targeting a 'cold' audience or those who have probably never heard of you before.

Here are five reasons to set the pixel as soon as possible on your website:

1. Track your site visitors.

You can use the pixel to track visitors to your website and their actions on your site. You can segment your visitors into separate custom audiences with this information.

For example, you can generate a custom audience of people who were on your website but didn't buy anything. You can create another custom audience of folks who added products to their cart but didn't buy. And finally, you can create a third audience of people who bought something from you successfully.

2. You can monitor your Facebook ad campaigns and optimize them.

When you optimize your advertisements, you can create ad campaigns that will lead to better ROI or return on investment for you. You no longer have to hope that someone will click on your ad, but you have real numbers to back you up, and then you can make informed decisions about the best way forward with your ad campaigns. With the Facebook pixel, you can understand which ads perform the best with which audiences.

3. Installing the Facebook pixel is free.

You don't have to pay for installing your pixel on Facebook. However, you need to pay Facebook when the time comes for you to use the pixel data. But just as we mentioned quite a few times, your pixel data comes from a warm audience, so these people are not strangers to your brand. Thanks to better audience targeting, if you install the pixel (unless you pay a developer to install the code for you), you have everything to gain and nothing to lose.

4. You can easily track standard or custom events on your website.

The Facebook pixel is split into two parts. The first part is the base code that you install in your site's global header—this means that the pixel will track ALL pages on your website. The second code is the code for events that you can add to your website's specific pages.

For example, you can add an event code to this if you want to track people who have signed up to your email list. You can also add an event code to if you're going to track people who clicked on the' add to cart' button. You can add an event code to your thank you or product delivery page if you want to track people who bought something.

5. The Facebook pixel is not limited to a single device or IP address.

If your website visitor logs into their Facebook account from a different computer or mobile device, the activity of that user can be tracked accurately. That's why even if visitors who checked your site from their desktop computer when they opened Facebook on a mobile device or tablet, they would still see your ads!

The Facebook pixel is, as you can see, very powerful. The capacity to track and evaluate a user's habits across your site is a marketing weapon you can utilize with Facebook ads. Install the pixel as soon as you read this chapter if you want to maximize your ad spend and get more conversions.

If you run an e-commerce store, the Facebook pixel will help you achieve your business goals faster while spending much less on advertising than when you advertise on other platforms. By adding just a few lines of code to your website, you have practically nothing to lose and everything to gain!

HOW TO CREATE YOUR FACEBOOK PIXEL

Creating the pixel is straightforward. You need to go to your **Facebook Ads Manager** (you learned how to do this in Chapter 2) and search for the **Pixels** tool. Keep in mind that you can only develop one pixel per ad account.

Here's a screenshot to help refresh your memory:

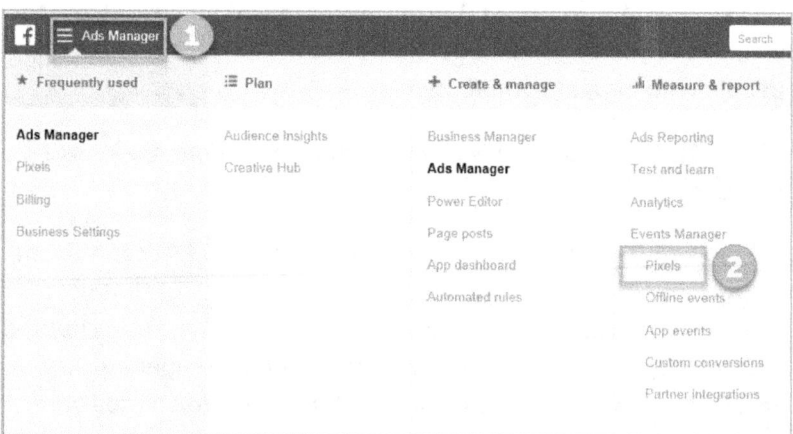

You will then see this on your screen:

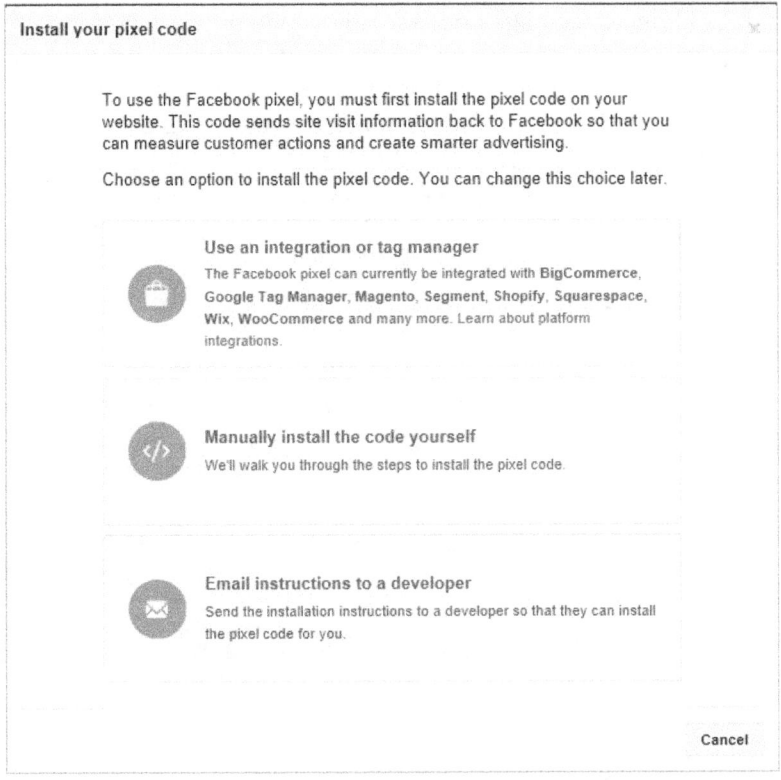

Carefully follow the on-screen instructions. Once you have the pixel set up on your website, you can create custom audiences and lookalike audiences based on your website's pixel data.

HOW TO APPLY PIXEL DATA FOR RETARGET MARKETING

Now that you know how powerful the combination of Facebook pixel and retarget marketing is, let's get into the nitty-gritty of how to leverage and take advantage of your audience data.

In the previous, we discussed custom audiences and lookalike audiences in considerable detail. In this section, we will quickly show you a sample application on how to use your pixel data for retargeting.

Create a Custom Audience Of People Who Have Visited Your Website

The pixel keeps track of people visiting your site over the past 180 days or 6 months. To target this audience, here's what you need to do:

1. Go to the **Ads Manager Menu,** to the **Assets** column and click on **Audiences.**

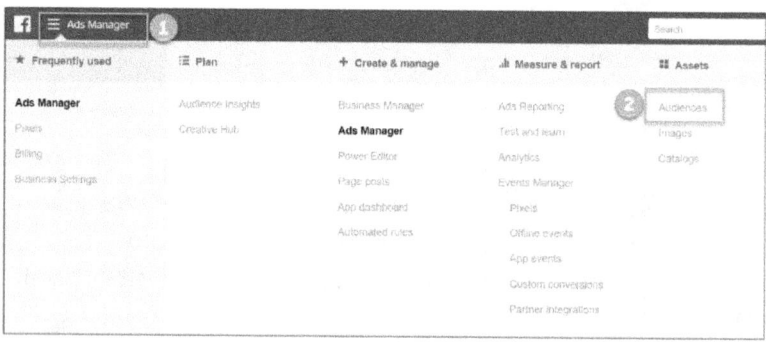

2. Next, click on the **Create a Custom Audience** button.

Reach the People Who Matter to You

Create and save audiences to reach the people who matter to your business. **Learn More**

Custom Audiences
Connect with the people who have already shown an interest in your business or product with Custom Audiences. You can create an audience from your customer contacts, website traffic or mobile app.

Create a Custom Audience

Lookalike Audiences
Reach new people who are similar to audiences you already care about. You can create a lookalike audience based on people who like your Page, conversion pixels or any of your existing Custom Audiences.

Create a Lookalike Audience

Saved audience
Save your commonly used targeting options for easy reuse. Choose your demographics, interests and behaviours, then save them to reuse in future ads.

Create a Saved Audience

3. Choose **Website Traffic** as shown below:

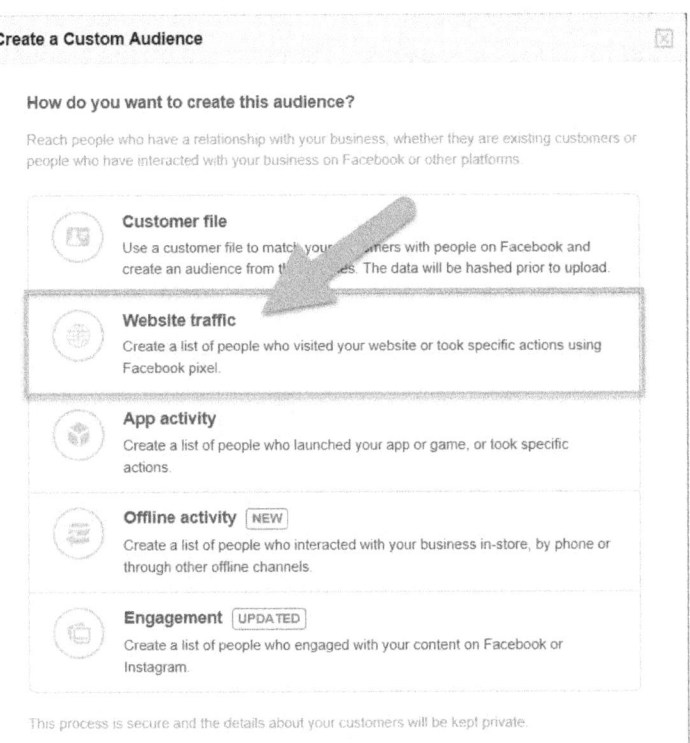

4. You can choose to target individuals who fulfill any or all of your criteria.

5. Choose whether you want to target all website visitors, people who visited specific pages, or target them by the amount of time they spent on your site.

6. You can do so by clicking on **Include More** or **Exclude** if you want to target a combination of any of these audiences or exclude some.

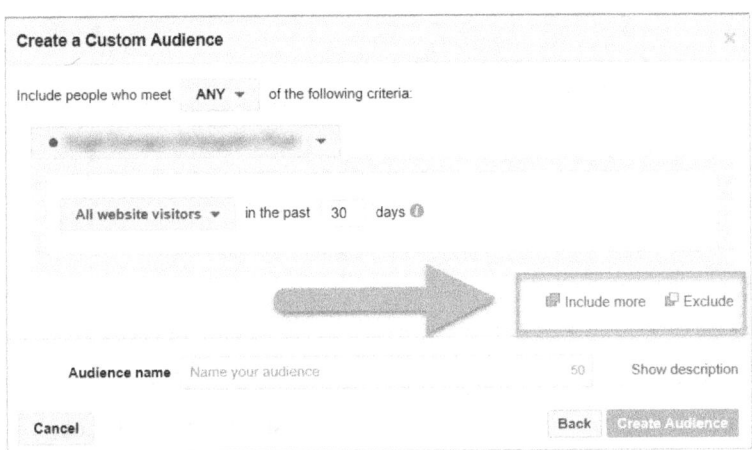

7. When you set up your custom audience details, you need to create an **Audience Name**. Make sure it's something that you can easily remember so you can identify the right audience when you create your ads.

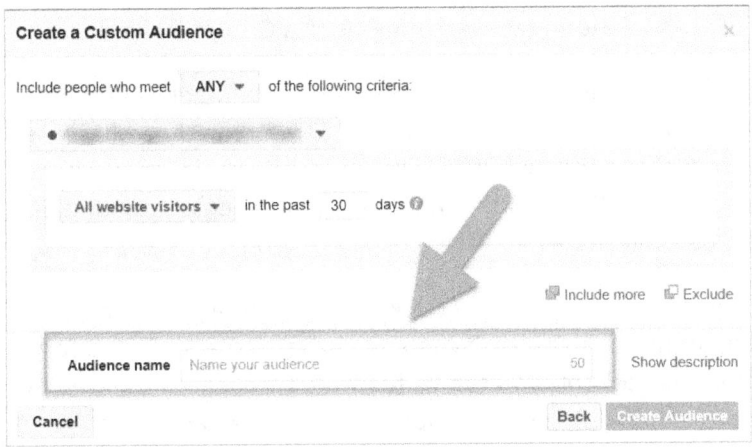

8. Click the **Create Audience** button to finalize your audience if you're happy with your custom audience.

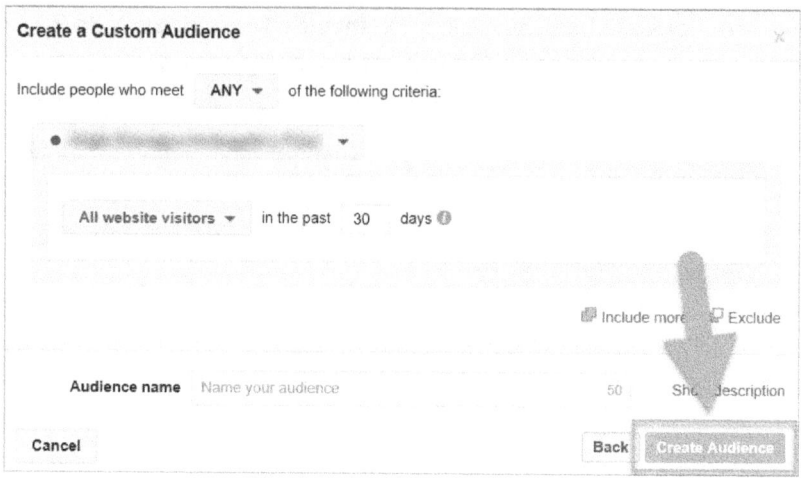

The targeting options are extensive on Facebook's custom audiences. Thanks to the pixel, no other platform can compete with the targeting level you can do with your Facebook ads. If you're still on the fence if it's worth taking the time to install such code on your website, you're going to leave a lot of money on the table. Tap into the behaviors of your audience and target them with today's all-powerful pixel!

Facebook Retarget Marketing Versus Google Remarketing

Not only is Facebook the platform that retargets visitors to the site. Sure it's not the only game in town to do that, but there's no doubt that because of the hyper-targeting choices you can do on Facebook, it's one of the most powerful. Google's remarketing is the best alternative to Facebook remarketing.

Remarketing by Google works almost the same way as remarketing by Facebook. Where Facebook remarketing ads are limited to Facebook, you can be followed throughout the web by Google remarketing! For example, if you read an article on Website 1, you will see an ad for Website 1 on these websites when you go to Websites 2 and 3, even though Websites 2 and 3 are entirely unrelated to Website 1!

The Facebook pixel's Google equivalent is known as the' Google Remarketing tag.' It's not a fancy name, but beginners can easily understand just what that code does. Essentially, it works the same way as the Facebook pixel that places the tag or code on pages you want to track.

When a website visitor lands on a 'cookied' page, it allows Google to follow you around the web, which is why you can see advertisements for Website 1 even though you left that site a long time ago.

What most marketers love about Google's remarketing is that click-through rates are significantly higher, resulting in a lower cost per click or action. Of course, with Facebook retargeting, the same thing is happening.

And the reason for this is because you're targeting people who have already interacted with your brand or your website with remarketing, whether it's on Google or Facebook. These people know you already—you need to make sure your ads remind them of who you are.

The main thing Google's remarketing has over Facebook is that Google's Display Network is quite extensive. So you can have your ad follow people around the web for as long as your budget lets you! In this case, advertising on Google may not be the most sensible thing to do, of course.

After all, if people have been continuously watching your ad for the past couple of days and have not taken any action, it could mean that they are not interested. They might also be able to develop this thing called 'ad blindness.'

The key takeaway is that whether you're using Facebook or Google to remarket to warm audiences, you need to create advertisements that will help them remember your brand. Create something exceptional, something to which they can relate. Do not follow them with annoying ads that do not speak to them and address their pain points.

FINAL THOUGHTS ABOUT RETARGET MARKETING

Retarget marketing is undoubtedly a potent tool in the arsenal of any serious marketer. If you want consistently high conversions, however, you will need to change your ads from time to time as well.

Keep your ads fresh and relevant, so your potential customers don't get annoyed. Keep in mind that annoyed users you aren't making any sales.

CHAPTER 7 - SPLIT TESTING YOUR FACEBOOK ADS FOR MAXIMUM PERFORMANCE

Split testing ads have many advantages, but most advertisers will not bother split testing their ads. Why is that? Because it's a lot of work and costly. But is it not worth the results? Let's find out in this chapter together!

What Is Split Testing?

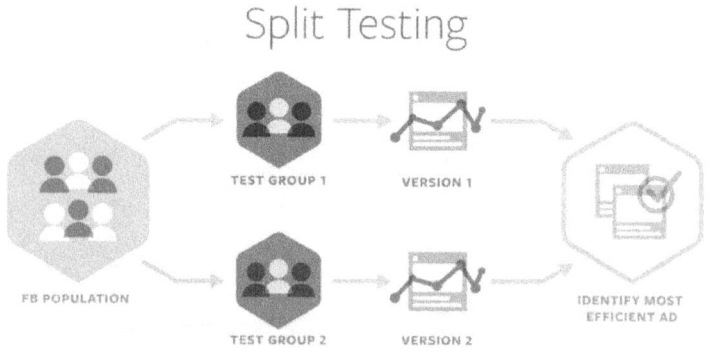

(Split testing in action. Image Source: Facebook.com)

Split testing, also called to as A / B testing, tests against each of 2 or more ad elements to find the best one to convert. It is a long process, especially if you want to test all aspects in your advertisement—from pictures to headline, description, placements, call-to-action, and more.

Successful Facebook marketers and advertisers will tell you that split testing their ads is their secret to success. By split testing, you can eliminate advertisements that do not result in good conversion numbers. When they scale their advertisements and target a broader audience, they use the highest converting ads by the end of their tests.

For example, you can do a three-way split test if you have three different audiences and want to see which audience will convert best for your ad. This means that Audience 1, Audience 2 and Audience 3 receive the same advertisement. You then look at the data that Facebook gives you after some time, and you can determine which audience responded best to that ad.

You can then create a lookalike audience with that knowledge to target other people with similar traits to the winning audience. So if Audience 1 wins the split test, you can create a lookalike audience of Audience 1. Not only does this increase your likelihood of success, but you know with 100 percent certainty that this particular ad is optimized for a specific audience.

WHAT BENEFITS COME FROM SPLIT TESTING?

In the early stages of a campaign, split testing will undeniably benefit those with the budget to burn through. Most ads will not convert—that's money down the drain. You can split up 100 ads, and you may not find a winning ad set until you launch the 101st ad.

That means you paid for nothing for the first 100 ads. But is this the truth? Obviously not. It merely means that you sifted through the dirt to find the gold nugget at the end. The winning ad set can pay for all the failed ads easily in most cases!

So here are some of the advantages of split testing and why you should start implementing this immediately in your Facebook ads:

1. There is no guessing – only pure, hard facts.

You eliminate many reasons why your ad is not successful with split testing. It's like a checklist. Ads 1 to 100 were unsuccessful, but Ad 101 is an astounding success. So you just literally crossed off your ad's 100 poor-converting variations. Also, split testing allows you to optimize your advertisement—you already know the elements that don't convert so you won't use it in your ad's next iteration.

2. Your results are both credible and tangible.

Who would say that 100 failed ads are not credible? You spent all that money to get to the end of the proverbial rainbow where the gold pot is. If someone asks you why your campaign was successful, you can easily say, "Oh, it's because I removed all the low-converting aspects of my ad and used only the highest converting elements to make a super successful ad." After so many failed tests, you can identify the exact recipe for your success!

3. Split testing is a very smart investment.

Most naysayers are going to say that split testing is like giving free cash to Facebook. While at the beginning it may be true, only one successful campaign can pay off all your failed ads. But what if you're not finding a successful campaign?

In terms of split testing, there are unlimited possibilities. You may not have found the right mix of good ad design and target audience. For instance, if you're promoting a lady's t-shirt and you're promoting an audience made up of men, then it's probably not surprising that you're getting weak conversions.

Split testing is only a smart investment if you have carefully considered all possible angles. Blindly approaching your advertising is not an intelligent strategy. It is better to have a solid campaign plan to help you find the ad set to win sooner rather than later.

4. You will discover a lot about your audience.

Once you understand what makes your audience tick or what motivates them to follow the call-to-action in your advertisement, you can try to offer similar products and services and expect good results.

For example, you know that a particular type of headline and image works best with a specific audience to get them to purchase Product A. You can then use similar elements in a future advertisement and connect with the same audience in the future to buy products related to Product A. There are really a lot of options you can explore once you know what your winning target audience will be.

BEST PRACTICES IN SPLIT TESTING

There is an infinite number of possibilities to perform your split testing. However, there are some common things for all split tests that usually lead to successful tests. Here are some of the best split testing practices:

1. Start testing vastly different aspects when you begin your campaign.

In the beginning, you don't just want to test the variation of one element. What you want to do is try to cover all possible bases, so you can get an overall understanding of what works for your audience. First, start with broad variables and use that element to narrow down your ad sets and do further split testing for each successful split test where one ad is the clear winner.

For example, if you're looking for the optimal age group to target, you might want to test an 18-30-year-old age group first and then a 30-50-year-old age group. Then, you can refine your experiment to look for a narrower age range once you have the winner for this test.

For instance, if the winner was the 18-30-year-old group, you can target users from 18-22, 23-26, and 27-30 in your next split test.

This strategy won't just save you money, but it also saves you time as testing multiple specific variations at once can take you from several days to a few weeks to get reliable data.

2. Change only one element and keep everything else the same.

This information is vital because you will not know which variable caused your ad to fail or succeed if you change many elements or variables in a split test. The elimination process is helpful as you go through each aspect and cross off those variables that are non-performing or non-converting.

You can run the same advertisement for two different audiences, for example. You will use the same image, headline, ad copy, and call-to-action, but the first audience will be in relationships between 18-25-year-old women, while the other audience will be single women aged 18-25. If one of the audiences comes out on top, then in your next ad campaign you know which audience group to target.

3. Run your split test ads for at least 3-4 days.

Facebook recommends that you allow your split tests to run for 3 to 14 days. Running tests for just 1-2 days may not produce enough data to determine a clear winner, and a 2-week trial is far too long and impractical for your budget. The advantage of allowing ads to run for a couple of days is that you can see which specific times of the day your audience engages with your ad. When optimizing your ad, you can then keep this variable in mind.

4. Have a sufficient budget in mind.

You should have a defined budget in mind before you start your tests; otherwise, you risk losing a fortune on Facebook ads. The bigger your audience, the larger the budget you need to allocate. The vital point to note here is that your budget should make it possible for Facebook to conduct the split test and establish a credible winner effectively.

Facebook will give you a suggested budget when setting up your ads, but often it can be quite expensive. Most experts on Facebook ads say you can start with a budget of $5/day for each ad set.

However, you need to increase your daily budget if you want to see results quickly. You should also be aware that you can choose to split the budget evenly or weigh one heavier than others.

HOW TO SPLIT TEST IN FACEBOOK ADS

We will give you a general overview of how to split Facebook ads testing in this section.

1. You need to go to the **Ads Manager** and **create a new ad** to start a split test campaign.

2. Decide on a **campaign objective.** Note that Facebook doesn't support split testing of all campaign objectives. Here's the full list of campaign objectives you can and cannot test:

- Brand awareness - no

- Reach - YES

- Traffic - YES

- Engagement - YES

- App installs - YES

- Video views - YES

- Lead generation - YES

- Messages - no

- Conversions - YES

- Catalog sales - YES

- Store visits – no

3. Tick the **'Create Split Test'** box once you have chosen an appropriate target. We chose **Traffic** as our goal of the campaign, as you can see in the screenshot below.

4. Create your **Campaign Name** and click '**Continue.**'

5. The next steps in the ad creation process will hinge on the variable that you choose to split test.

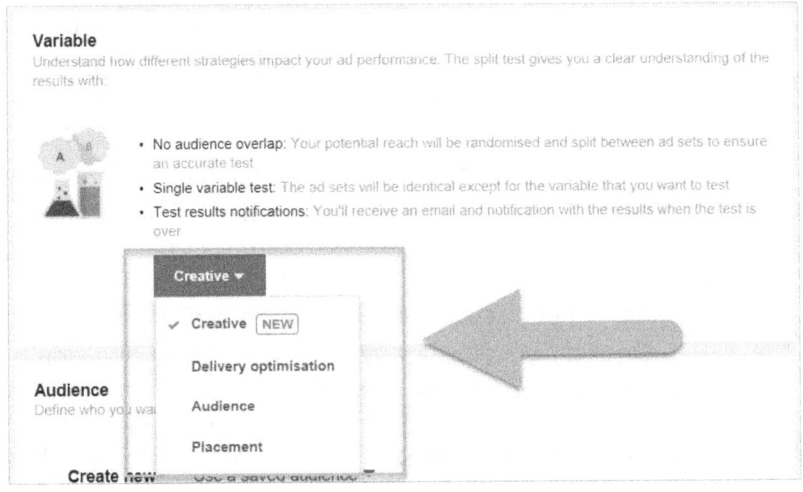

As you can see in the above screenshot, you can split test into four main variable categories. These are the following:

- **Creative** – The image, headline, ad text and so on can be experimented and split test. For example, you can split a single image ad from a video ad. You can also try using the same image with different headlines.

- **Delivery optimization** – Decide whether you want to split test between link clicks, landing page views, impressions, or unique daily reach. For example, by optimizing one ad for conversions, you can split test and optimize the second ad for link clicks.

- **Audience** – You can split test based on the audience's location, gender, interests, age, relationship status, level of education, buying behaviors and even test custom audiences among your audience. For example, you can show one ad to a group of Seattle-based women and then show the same to a second group of Toronto-based women.

- **Placement** – Split test where ads are to be displayed (mobile, desktop, newsfeed, right column, Instagram, Audience Network, and so forth). For example, if you want custom placements versus automatic placements, you can test them. You can also compare mobile placements against desktop placements.

Choose the variable you want to split test. Once you've set up your advertisements, Facebook will then record and compare the results. Once the winning advertisement is determined, you'll receive a notification email with your split test results on it.

This information can then be used to move forward with the next split-test (for example, further narrowing down the variables you want to test), or to design your next ad campaign and refine your overall advertising strategy.

FINAL THOUGHTS

The mantra of successful marketers on Facebook is "always test, test, test." Yes, it can get expensive, but a successful split test often leads to impressive ROIs!

Very few marketers attribute their success to luck–almost all of them credit split testing as the reason for their success. The numbers, as the saying goes, do not lie!

CHAPTER 8: BOOST YOUR PROFITS WITH FACEBOOK DYNAMIC ADS

Facebook Ads is a powerful marketing platform. However, Facebook Ads cannot determine buying intent compared to keyword-based advertising on search engines because users do not usually go to Facebook to search for things to buy.

By introducing dynamic ads, Facebook came up with a way to circumvent this inherent weakness. Many advertisers have been won over compared to the usual static ads by the impressive results they get from dynamic ads. In this chapter, we'll show you how using Facebook dynamic ads so you too can boost your profits!

What Are Dynamic Ads?

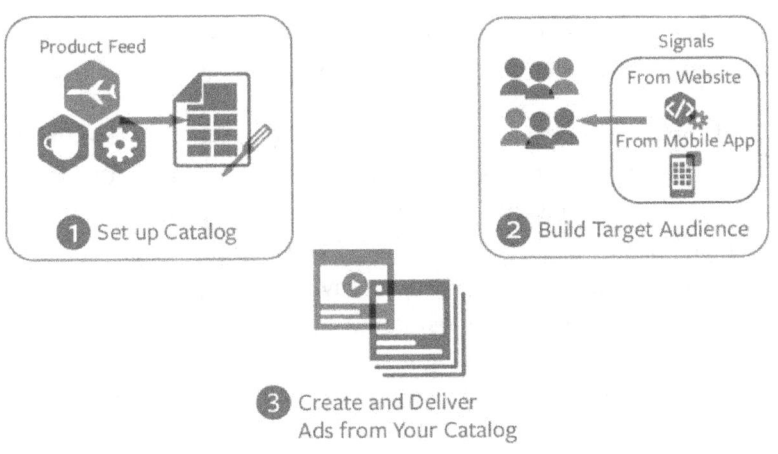

(Facebook Dynamic Ads. Image Source: Facebook.com)

Dynamic ads are Facebook ds that are merely automated. Some marketing experts call it "retargeting ads on steroids." It targets people on your website or app and sends them ads based on what they did on your website.

The Facebook pixel tracks their actions, and your dynamic ads will come into play in a fully automated manner when they go on Facebook.

If you have an online store and sell tens of thousands of products, you can upload your product catalog to Facebook instead of creating an advertisement for each product. Imagine just how many hours you save with dynamic ads!

The only real work that you and your team need to do is to ensure that your catalog is up to date and contains all the relevant product details. Once you set up your ad template and set your budget, it's almost a hands-off advertising machine!

For instance, your pixel tracks when a customer views or adds a product to his cart. Your pixel will know it when they buy that product. When they go to Facebook, the system will know precisely what that customer did on your website.

If they viewed a product but didn't buy it, they will see an ad on their news feed or wherever you choose to display your dynamic ads for the same product. Likewise, if that customer purchased that product, they will NOT see an ad on Facebook for that product (that would be very annoying!). They're going to see another product on display instead. And since they've already bought from you, they know you and will most likely buy from you again, especially if they had an excellent first product experience.

Dynamic ads also help to circumvent blindness. With so many ads overrunning people's news feeds, it's no surprise that many people are developing banner ad blindness. With dynamic ads, however, your ads are so relevant and timely. After all, they just looked at that particular product 10 minutes ago, causing people to feel more compelled to buy your ad on site!

In short, Facebook dynamic ads are an incredibly clever way to retarget your customers by providing them with highly relevant ads wherever they are in the sales funnel!

How To Get Started With Facebook Dynamic Ads

Initially setting up dynamic ads may be difficult. If you want to save time and resources on a long-term basis, however, you must invest some time and money, so your dynamic ads will run smoothly in the future.

Getting started with dynamic ads, you'd need the following:

1. The Facebook Pixel

From reading in previous chapters, you know the key to generating custom audiences and maximizing your ROI is the

Facebook pixel. The pixel plays another essential role in dynamic ads in helping you to boost your profits further.

If you already set up the base pixel code on your website, you should edit or modify the custom audience pixel. Dynamic ads require three Custom Data events, and you need to edit the pixel code on your website for these three events:

- **Product pages** (event name is **View Content**) – The code will report the product IDs that were viewed from the catalog.

- **Add to cart pages** (event name is **Add to Cart**) – The code will report the product IDs added to the shopping cart.

- **Purchase confirmation pages** (event name is **Purchase**) – The code identifies the product IDs purchased.

Here is what the *View Content* pixel event looks like:

```
<!-- Custom Audience Pixel Code -->
<script>
!function(f,b,e,v,n,t,s){if(f.fbq)return;n=f.fbq=function(){n.callMethod?
n.callMethod.apply(n,arguments):n.queue.push(arguments)};if(!f._fbq)f._fbq=n;
n.push=n;n.loaded=!0;n.version='2.0';n.queue=[];t=b.createElement(e);t.async
t.src=v;s=b.getElementsByTagName(e)[0];s.parentNode.insertBefore(t,s)}(windo
document,'script','//connect.facebook.net/en_US/fbevents.js');
// Insert Your Custom Audience Pixel ID below.
fbq('init', '<FB_PIXEL_ID>');

fbq('track', 'ViewContent', {
  content_name: 'Really Fast Running Shoes',
  content_category: 'Apparel & Accessories > Shoes',
  content_ids: ['1234'],
  content_type: 'product',
  value: 0.50,
  currency: 'USD'
});

</script>
<!-- End Custom Audience Pixel Code -->
```

(Image Source: Facebook.com)

If the code looks intimidating to you, it's best to get an experienced developer's help to make sure there are no code errors.

2. Facebook SDK

You can integrate the Facebook SDK into your iOS, Android or web app to target your app users with dynamic ads if you have a mobile app or plan to have one. Like the website Facebook pixel, you also need to integrate the three events you need to add to your app (View Content, Add To Cart, and Purchase).

Here's an example code for an iOS app event:

```
[FBSDKAppEvents logEvent:FBSDKAppEventNameAddedToCart
    valueToSum:54.23
    parameters:@{
    FBSDKAppEventParameterNameCurrency    : @"USD",
    FBSDKAppEventParameterNameContentType : @"product",
    FBSDKAppEventParameterNameContentID   : @"123456789"
    }
];
```

If all that alphanumeric code makes your head spin, please get help from a qualified mobile app developer (like you can get from Focused Idea at https://focusedidea.com) to help ensure that your dynamic ads are running correctly.

3. Business Manager

It's free and easy to get a business manager account. You can add your business manager pages and ad accounts, and allocate specific roles to others. It also makes all your assets easy to manage in one place.

4. Facebook Page

When you launch dynamic ads, your business needs a Facebook page. It's going to represent your business on Facebook.

5. Product Catalog

The last essential component to make your dynamic ads run successfully is the Facebook product catalog. It is the virtual database of your business on Facebook. It is an inventory of all the products that you want to promote on Facebook. For all your products, you can upload one data feed, or you can upload multiple data feeds, particularly if your business operates in more than one country or has numerous divisions.

You can create a catalog by going to your **Business Manager Menu > Assets > Catalogs**.

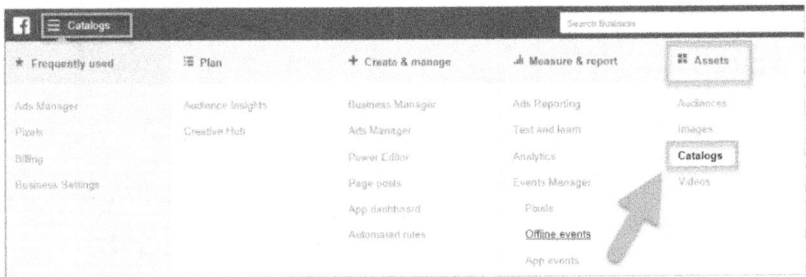

These are the different catalog types you can create:

- **E-commerce** – You can upload the data feed of all your products to your catalog if you have an e-commerce store. If you already have a shopping product feed from Shopify, WooCommerce, Magento, BigCommerce, or Google, you can set up your catalog faster just by using the Facebook Feed plugin.

- **Travel** – upload a data feed of vacation properties, hotels, flights, and destinations.

- **Real estate** – create a catalog of rental properties and real estate listings.

- **Auto** – Create a vehicle and vehicle catalog for your automotive business.

Once you have created your catalog, you need to create a data feed containing all the information you want to advertise in your dynamic ads. For each type of catalog, the required item information will vary, and you need to use the required format and file type of Facebook to create a proper data feed.

Now that you know the essential requirements to get started with dynamic ads, go to the next section where we're going to discuss how to launch your dynamic ads and the best practices to do that.

HOW TO CREATE AND START A DYNAMIC AD CAMPAIGN

You must have all the requirements we mentioned in the previous section up and running to create a dynamic ad. You may not be able to complete the creation of a dynamic ad otherwise.

1. The first thing you need to do to create a dynamic ad is to ensure that you choose Catalog Sales as your marketing or campaign objective.

What's your marketing objective? Help: Choosing an objective

Awareness	Consideration	Conversion
Brand Awareness	Traffic	Conversions
Reach	Engagement	Catalogue Sales
	App Installs	Store Visits
	Video Views	

2. In the next section, select the Catalog you want to use and name your campaign name (or use the default name).

3. To set up your **ad set**, follow the next steps. Choose the right **product set** to advertise. Then set up your audience (who you want to show the ads to), **placement** (where your dynamic ads will be displayed), **budget** (how much you want to spend per day or for your campaign's lifetime), and **schedule** (how long you want the campaign to run).

4. Set the **format** of your **ad** in the ad section. You can use choose between carousel ad, a single image ad, or a collection ad.

5. Finally, set up your ad creative template in the Links section and preview how your dynamic ad will look. Here's a preview sample:

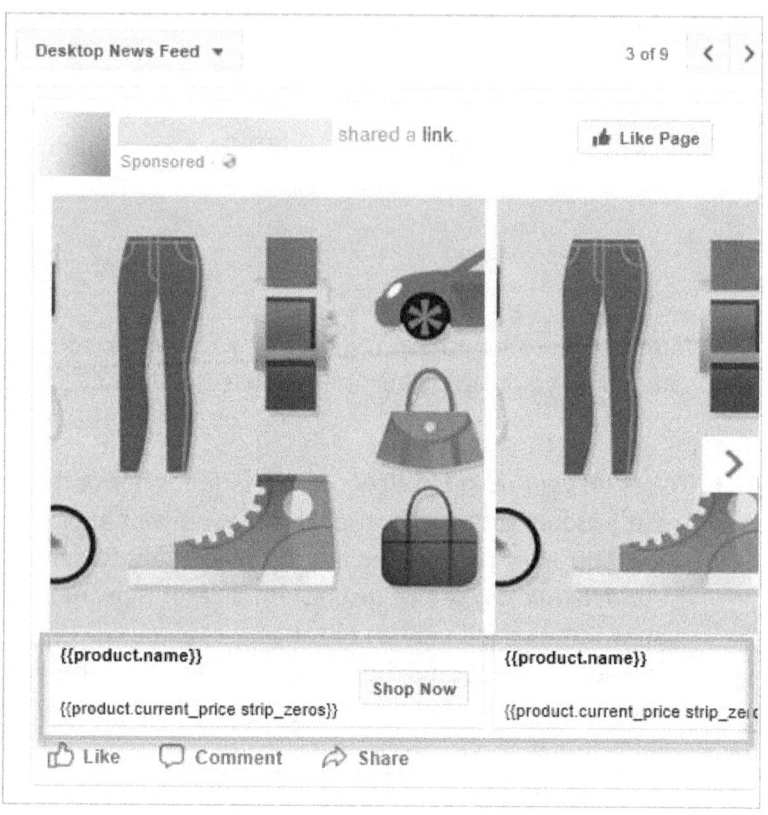

Double check your work and make sure you're happy with how your dynamic ads will be displayed. Remember your ads will be dynamically and automatically served, so you need to make sure that all the elements of a good ad are still in place in the data feed of your catalog.

HOW FACEBOOK DYNAMIC ADS CAN BOOST YOUR PROFITS

Remarket targeting is a powerful advertising strategy as you target a "warm" or "hot" audience. Not only do you retarget these audiences with Facebook dynamic ads, but you also show them dynamic ads relevant to what they've done on your website or app! Apart from this significant benefit, let's go through a few more points about how dynamic ads can boost your profits:

1. You spend less time creating and editing ads.

You only have to create your ad once with dynamic ads. You define the product variables that you want to use in your ad, and Facebook will pull the data from your data feed automatically.

You don't need to set up a reminder on your calendar to help you remember that some of your ads need to update the pricing – you can edit your data feed, and then Facebook will use that.

If you want to update a product image, you need to update the link in the data feed. You also don't need to update the inventory levels manually, so if you run out of stock, your pixel will know it, and Facebook won't serve that particular product's dynamic ad.

2. Spend more time growing your business.

Dynamic ads will help you efficiently grow your business. You will have a lot of free time on your hands once set up your catalog and your ad creative. You can use this to find new avenues or platforms for reaching your target audience.

Since the primary intent of dynamic ads is for people who have interacted with your business, you can then focus on reaching out to "cold" audiences or people who have not previously interacted with your site or app.

3. Offer personalized recommendations.

Since the Facebook pixel can track the actions of your customers on your site or app, your ad will dynamically display the product that your they looked at or added to their cart but did not purchase. Your dynamic ad will not show them the same product for those who have already purchased an item from you. Instead, a different product will upsell or cross-sell your dynamic ad.

4. Improve your conversion rates.

Ideally, you would want a 100% conversion rate from your ads. But doing this is nearly impossible, as too many factors come into play during the purchasing process. The retargeting system from Facebook helped to increase conversion rates for many advertisers.

But with dynamic ads, retargeting has been taken to an entirely different level. Because of this, many advertisers are reporting impressive conversion rates and massive profits!

FINAL WORDS

Facebook dynamic ads are an improvement over retarget marketing. Not everybody can produce dynamic ad campaigns, though. For now, this option is available only to companies that have a product inventory to sell.

If you're marketing a couple of items, you can still remarket to your customers, just not at the scale and ease of dynamic advertisements.

CHAPTER 9: HOW TO LOWER YOUR OVERALL FACEBOOK AD BUDGET

On Facebook Ads, you can set your budget. You can go as low as $1 a day, a couple of hundred dollars or go as high as you like. If you want to get the best conversion rates and reach the right audience, however, you would have to spend more than a dollar a day.

Even if you have the cash to burn, you don't want to spend too much, because it's just not a very wise business decision.

After all, the reason you're advertising on Facebook for smart business owners and marketers is so you can get the highest conversion rates at the lowest possible price. If you think you're spending too much and you'd like to know how to lower your overall budget for Facebook Ads, keep reading this chapter.

HOW TO MAKE THE MOST OF YOUR FACEBOOK AD BUDGET

You would need to have some rules in place first before you set up your advertisement on Facebook. You need to identify your campaign goals, your target audience, your ad schedule, and so much more. You also need to have some key metrics in place, so you know whether or not your campaign is profitable.

Ideally, you should know where each dollar of your ad spending goes so that you don't throw money away. If your campaign is in the red, you have to figure out how to optimize your campaign so that you end up in the black.

Here are a few techniques that will help you get the most out of your ad budget:

1. Set a target revenue.

Revenue means real and tangible dollars. It does not mean page likes and comments on your ad that went viral. While ad engagement is a useful metric, you want to get enough revenue at the end of the day to make a healthy profit.

For instance, if you want to make $10,000 in revenue for your week-long campaign and the price of your product is $100, you need to make at least 100 sales in 7 days. Then you can work backward and estimate how much your ad budget should be to make at least 100 sales.

2. Set up the Facebook events pixel code on your website.

If you want to track what your site visitors are doing after going to your website from Facebook, you need to have the pixel installed. Set up the events you'd like to track. As an example, if you want to track how many people have bought your $100 product, then you can track download or thank you page. The pixel will record it as a lead or sale each time someone lands on that page. Knowing this data allows you to adjust your budget as your campaign progresses.

3. Plan out your ad campaign.

Use the correct campaign objective to help Facebook optimize your ad for you. The Facebook algorithm is advanced, and it can be used by advertisers to maximize their investment. Some goals will result in higher conversion costs while others may result in lower conversion costs. Set the right target to help you work within your budget.

4. Monitor your results and adjust your campaign as needed.

You're not setting your ad budget in stone. It can be adjusted whenever you see the need. The reporting tool on Facebook is accurate and takes place in real time, so you know that you make business decisions based on time-sensitive data.

You may want to scale your ads or increase your audience size if you see that you are underspending. Then double down on ads that return a profit for you and deactivate the rest if you're overspending.

HOW TO LOWER YOUR OVERALL FACEBOOK AD SPEND

There are several techniques that you can use to reduce your total ad spending. Some of the tips we'll share in this chapter may work for you, while some may not. But the only way you can find out if any of these tips are going to help you with your budget is to try them out.

1. Know your target audience.

Don't just randomly target everyone in a particular location. You can hyper-target people with Facebook Ads in a way not available on other advertising platforms. If you're in a niche business, you ought to have an idea of who your target clients are. The narrower your target audience, the easier it is for you to create advertisements that resonate with that audience.

For instance, if you sell women's fishing accessories, you may want to exclude men from your audience. You can then create separate advertisements for each age group and then design your ads in such a way that your audience thinks the product has been made specifically for them. When you make your advertisement relevant, the higher the chances that that customer will click on your ad and purchase your product.

2. Set a bid cap.

You can set a bid cap per link click and per 1,000 impressions on the ad set level in the **Budget & Schedule** section. A bid cap helps you to control your bid and ensure that you don't go beyond your allotted budget per action. For example, if you have a $20 daily budget and you're paying per link click, you can set a $1 bid cap per click, so you know you'll get at least 20 clicks a day.

Facebook can cost you $2 or $4 per click, or even more if you don't set a bid cap. So when you create your ad, it's best to use this feature. Keep in mind that if your bid cap is too low, it may not be competitive and your ad may not be displayed to your target audience.

3. Make sure there's no audience overlap.

When you have overlapping audiences, you're essentially going to be bidding against yourself. For instance, if you are targeting freelancers, a small part of your audience may also be entrepreneurs.

Audience overlap means you bid twice to show the same audience your ads. The good thing is that Facebook won't let you compete with yourself, but it can drive up costs. Ultimately, having overlapping audiences can lead to spending your budget inefficiently.

To check that your audiences don't overlap, go to **Ads Manager > Audiences**, then check the boxes next to the audiences that you want to compare. Click **Actions > Show Audience Overlap**. You will see something like this:

Audience Overlap

Choose an audience and compare the number of people and the overlap with up to four other audiences.

Selected Audience		My Audience ⊕

My Audience
2,000,000 people

Comparison Audiences		Overlap	% Overlap of Selected Audience
My Other Audience 155,000,000 people		1,500,000 people	75%

Show Add Another Audience

4. Always split test your ads.

Earlier we covered all the details on how to split test. Just remember that split testing will not only save you time, it will also help you save money as you already know what does NOT work. Split testing helps you narrow down your choices to find the winning combination of audience, placement, and ad creative.

5. Retarget people who have been on your website or app.

Retarget marketing works as I shared previously. It works because you don't target cold audiences directly. Instead, you target people who have already visited your website, your mobile app, and even people who have gone to visit your brick-and-mortar location.

Facebook makes creating custom audiences easy for you, so you're showing your ads to people who've seen your products and even bought from you. They know your business to some extent already. Knowing you increases their likelihood of doing business with you as opposed to a total stranger who has never heard of you before.

6. Refresh your ad creatives.

You may want to consider your ad creatives if you notice a trend of more expensive ad costs. If you have been using the same image for several weeks and the same ad has been shown ten times to the same audience, they are likely to have developed ad blindness already.

They don't *see* your ad anymore, so you need to think about another way to try to get their attention. Alternatively, if you don't respond to your target audience, you might target the wrong audience.

7. Use video ads.

If a picture paints a thousand words, video plays a thousand pictures. Thanks to video ads, many advertisers report very low ad costs. People engage in video ads because they don't have to read a lot of text, and it's easier to consume video than other media.

Billions of video views happen every day on Facebook. Facebook is now literally on the verge of overtaking YouTube as the most prominent video platform any day, so you should take advantage of it and use video ads.

One strategy successful marketers use is to create video ads–nothing fancy, just an iPhone-shot video where they're talking to camera prospects and showing their products in action.

All you have to do is get creative. You should have an idea of your audience's likes and dislikes if you've studied your target market, hit their pain points, and offer your solution.

8. Let your ads run for a few days or a few weeks to optimize.

If you only run your ads for 1 or 2 days, your ad costs are likely to be relatively higher. Don't be anxious. Instead, allow Facebook the opportunity to optimize your ad and reach your target audience. If you have an audience of 1,000,000 and you run a $5/day campaign, then in 1-2 days you won't reach that 1,000,000.

Facebook gives you an estimated reach or estimate of the daily outcome for your campaign when you set up your budget. Once your ad has been optimized, and more people are engaging with your ad, you can expect to pay lower ad costs.

9. Use powerful words in your ad copy.

The headline of your advertisement should immediately catch the attention of your reader. If you sell a product that solves a particular problem, mention it in the headline. Do not hide the main benefit of your product on your landing page. Rather, reel them with powerful words that resonate with them and get them to click on your ad and follow your call-to-action.

10. Give away freebies.

If you want people to engage with your ad, give them anything for free. It may sound like you're tricking people, but if you're going to get more leads and customers, you've got to give them something worth it for free.

If you sell a high-priced product or service, consider gratuitously giving away a small item. Or offer a discount. Give your audience an incentive to click on your ad, and Facebook will reward you with lower ad costs.

11. Try advertising outside of peak sale seasons.

You will experience higher ad cost during certain times of the year. This is particularly true during Christmas, Thanksgiving, Black Friday, Valentine's Day, and other distinguished holidays. People spend and buy things online at these times of the year.

So it's natural for marketers to want to put their brands and products in front of the buying crowd. When more advertisers compete, everybody's ad costs increase; consider advertising outside of these peak seasons if you want to lower your budget.

FINAL WORDS

Just because you can advertise for $1 or $2 a day on Facebook doesn't mean you should stick to this year-round rock-bottom budget. With such a budget, you won't get far. You need to spend some money if you want to make the most of Facebook ads.

In this chapter, the tips and techniques I have shared should help you reach your target audience without breaking the bank. Test each method and see what works best for you, helping you to reduce your total spending on Facebook ads.

CHAPTER 10: HOW TO CREATE A FACEBOOK LEAD CAPTURE FUNNEL

You'll hear the words "lead generation funnel" or "sales funnel" wherever you go in the marketing world, whether it's online or offline marketing. But what exactly do these terms mean? And why do you need to know what a funnel is and how it works?

Well, read on because you will learn all about the lead funnel in this chapter, mainly how to use Facebook Ads to create the perfect lead capture funnel for your business.

WHAT IS A LEAD CAPTURE FUNNEL?

It is essential that all of your customers and customers go through a sales funnel, regardless of the product or service you offer.

You need to know every step of the funnel so that you can guide your customers through it and take them to the bottom of the funnel where the product purchase takes place. A lead capture funnel will guide your lead from being a *potential customer* to being a *paying customer*.

Here's a good example of what a sales funnel or a lead capture looks like:

While many marketers call the different funnel stages by different names, the idea is the same. Let's go through each stage here:

- At the **top of the funnel** (ToFu), your prospects are complete and total strangers to your business. They don't know who you are, but they found you through social media or a Google search or wherever. You want them to know about your business at this point and what you can do for them.

  For example, if you're selling weight loss supplements, you want people at the top of the funnel to know your brand is there, so offer them something of value to help them keep your brand in their minds.

- You try to convert your visitors from being strangers to becoming leads at the next stage of the funnel—the middle of the funnel (MoFu). You want them to consider your business seriously at this point for whatever pain you may be able to help them with or provide a solution.

  You want your potential customers to start engaging with your brand by hooking them in with valuable posts, ebooks, white papers, and more at this stage to continue our previous example. In short, distinguish your brand from your competitors.

- Your leads are ready to convert from potential customers to paying customers at the **bottom of the funnel** (BoFu). Since you've already gained their trust, this is the best time to ask for the sale.

- Finally, as you can see in the sample funnel image above, once you have converted your leads into customers and provide them with excellent services or products, they will help create buzz around your brand by promoting you to their networks.

Although there are several methods that you can use to drive your visitors from the top of the funnel to the bottom, we will focus on using Facebook every step of the way in this chapter. We will discuss the various ad strategies you can use to create a successful lead capture funnel on Facebook.

WHY ARE LEAD FUNNELS IMPORTANT?

It is crucial to understand how a lead funnel works to optimize your advertisements for your potential customers' sales journey. If you target a cold audience, for example, they'd be at the top of the funnel.

They don't know you, and they don't trust you, so they're most likely not going to buy from you if you're trying to sell them something.

This concept is particularly true for high-ticket products that require a relatively large investment – say from a few hundred to several thousand dollars.

If you sell a product that is relatively cheap and does not require too much thinking, you can probably make some sales to a cold audience. If your price range fits within an impulsive buyer's budget and your target audience has a large number of impulse buyers, then you're off to make some substantial profits even with top customers of the funnel!

How To Structure Your Funnel And The Right Ads To Use

We will cover a few strategies in this section that you can use to move your leads from being a potential customer to a paying buyer.

Top Of The Funnel Facebook Ad Strategies *(Awareness)*

You want people to get to know more about your brand or business at the top of your sales funnel. You want to gain their confidence, and you want to appear to be an authority in your niche.

The best way to connect with a cold audience is by using the following campaign goals:

- Brand Awareness

- Reach

You're letting people know you exist with these goals and you're setting your presence in their minds. Give them something of value to remind them of you.

You should also add the Facebook pixel to your website at this point. The pixel will begin to track people landing on your site, and you can then retarget them in the sales funnel later.

The pixel plays an enormous role in your sales funnel's success so make sure you set it up properly. You should also add events to relevant pages to allow you to segment your audience further and later target the most appropriate people.

The number of people you reach with your Brand Awareness ad will depend on the size and budget of your target audience. The larger your budget, the faster you can get your ad in front of a large number of people, and the more people you have at the top of your sales funnel.

You may get lucky in some cases and have some sales here and there from your Brand Awareness and Reach ads. But at this point, conversion rates are generally low. Again, you're just introducing yourself to your target market—you're not selling anything.

In real life, people who try to sell something to us the first time we meet them turn most of us off. Generally speaking, we think people who do this are sleazy salespeople, and we tend to keep our distance from such people. To use another analogy, think of this process as your "first date" with your potential customer.

Middle of Funnel Facebook Ad Strategies *(Consideration)*

In the middle of your funnel, the people you are targeting already know of your brand. After all, this is your "second date" or even the third, fourth, or fifth date (this depends on how your funnel is structured).

In the previous stage, you introduced yourself and offered them something worthwhile, and now it's time to get them to consider your business. At this point, the marketing goals you should choose are:

- Traffic

- Engagement

- App installs

- Video views

- Lead generation

- Messages

We covered these various goals in detail in the first chapter. The most important thing to remember is that you must continue to give your leads plenty of value at this stage so that they will move on to the next stage—the bottom of the funnel.

If you give something of value to people, they will be more willing to click on your ads to visit your website. They will also engage with your posts and page, install your app, view your videos, fill out your generation lead form, and send inquiries and messages to you on Facebook.

At this stage, should you ask for the sale? You can, of course. Don't expect vast amounts of sales, though. Your leads are still getting to know you, some may trust you already, and at this stage, some may be willing to part with their cash. But most of them are still not going to buy anything from you. To encourage them to move down to the bottom of the funnel, you will need to work a little more.

Bottom of Funnel Facebook Ad Strategies *(Conversions)*

You have done great work on the top, and middle stages of your sales funnel. Now comes the fun part –asking people to buy. At this point, you ask people to decide to commit to your business as either a one-time customer or as a subscriber.

Continuing with the analogy of dating, you're asking your leads to commit with you in a relationship. You gained their trust, and they got to know you very well over the previous "dates." You can ask them to commit and give you their money in exchange for your product or service with just a little more push and persistence.

This stage is also known as the Conversion stage because you are asking your leads to convert from potential customers to paying customers. Facebook makes it simple to choose the best campaign objectives for your bottom of the funnel leads; these are:

- Conversions

- Catalog Sales

- Store Visits

Facebook already knows the behaviors of your leads and will help you optimize your ad for higher conversion rates. Facebook can only do so much, though. To sway your leads to your side, you have to use some very persuasive copy and ad materials.

No matter how interested your leads are, and no matter how engaged they are with your ads, if you don't give them an incentive to sign up or buy from you, you're not likely to get any sales.

Most experts suggest using testimonials from customers and product demos to convert your leads. Testimonials or endorsements are compelling because they help to assure your leads that you are trustworthy. Testimonials will help to ease their minds that you're not going to take their money and run, and they'll get the product exactly as advertised.

On the other hand, product demos help assure your leads that your products will work. If you're selling a kitchen product, you want to show your leads precisely how they can use the product.

If you can use your product outside the kitchen, make a demo video. Show all the possible uses of your product in real life. Make your leads see the value they will get by investing or purchasing your product.

When you've painted a compelling picture of your product in your leads' minds, converting and buying from you will be easier for them. You will get people buying from your website, on your app, or in your store(s) in no time at all. Not only will you get higher conversion rates, but Facebook may also reward you with lower ad costs.

WHAT'S NEXT AFTER CREATING A SUCCESSFUL LEAD FUNNEL?

It will take quite a bit of hard work and probably a lot of money to get your leads from top to bottom of your sales funnel. But your work doesn't stop there. Facebook Ads may help you capture and turn your leads into customers, but you'd still have to provide excellent service to your customers at the end of the day.

If you've invested a lot in getting people to buy your product, you better make sure your it works. Nowadays, there are far too many sleazy salesmen trying to make a quick buck from unsuspecting customers–don't be one of them!

> *Provide excellent service to your customers, give them excellent value for their money, and you will soon have plenty of testimonials and social evidence.*

What can you do with glowing testimonials from satisfied customers? You can use them, of course, in your next round of Facebook Ads! If you have hundreds or thousands of satisfied customers, scaling up your business is much easier.

Your satisfied customers will help spread the word about your business, and you'll have even more people at the top of your sales funnel. Thanks to Facebook Ads, your business will be growing at top speed, and you might soon be dominating your niche!

CONCLUSION: FINAL THOUGHTS ON FACEBOOK ADS

There are many "ingredients" that make Facebook advertisements successful and highly converting. Put in some time to learn how the platform works and look up techniques of how other successful marketers advertise on Facebook.

You may not learn everything you need to know in a few weeks or even a few months. But once you get the hang of Facebook Ads, creating ads that capture not only the attention of your audience, but also their loyalty, and of course their money will be relatively easy and fast for you.

Here's to your success!

ABOUT THE AUTHOR

Like you, author and business owner Brian Gibbs understands the continual need to find new customers and clients.

Throughout his 20+ years of building websites and providing digital marketing services, and more importantly, real-life, in-the-trenches business experience, his approach to getting clients challenges tradition. Brian appreciates, and shares with listeners, that knowing the best and most cost-effective places to find clients is more challenging than ever. He also understands that it doesn't have to be.

Brian is a recognized digital marketing expert and strategist. He has had the opportunity to work with businesses of all sizes in various industries from around the world to implement successful marketing strategies that helped them all see positive gains.

Prior to launching his digital marketing career, Brian was an elite athlete who competed on the U.S. National Cycling team, raced in several National Championship and Olympic Trials. He brings that drive and dedication to everything he does still, today.

NOTES